Akademie der Wissenschaften der DDR
Zentralinstitut fuer Kybernetik und Informationsprozesse

# KNOWLEDGE BASED PROGRAM CONSTRUCTION (2)

*Rainer Hesse and Reinhard Klette*

Berlin, December 1988

Herausgegeben vom
Zentralinstitut für Kybernetik und
Informationsprozesse (ZKI)
der Akademie der Wissenschaften der DDR
Kurstraße 33
Berlin, 1086
DDR
Druckgenehmigungs-Nr.: III-12-12 Ag 521/437/89
ISSN 0232-8127

## ABSTRACT

The paper describes a knowledge based approach to problem oriented construction of domain specific software. A knowledge based program construction system is vertically stratified into the target level, the design level and the strategy level. The system performs the hierarchical planning of programs by scheduling operators of the design space for automatic and user controlled refinement and specification of the program to be constructed.

Horizontally, the system is stratified into problem space, program space and inference machine.

A problem space and a program space are used for modelling the programming task and the program to be constructed, respectively. The target level representation consists of a problem space data base accumulating a specification of the programming task, a program space knowledge base containing knowledge of how to construct programs, and a connection table of the inference machine which determines relations between problem and program space.

The representation language of the program space is defined by program schemes. The knowledge of this space consists of rules describing transformations for hierarchical refinement of program schemes. Constraint processing is used to consider interdependencies between operators and operands of the program space.

The problem space is characterized by a relational data base and a data base manager which collects the problem specification via user dialogues, and by conclusions derived from these data.

Reasoning on conditions is used for communicating between the problem and the program space where a connection table is used for storing cross relations.

*Keywords:* program construction, program synthesis,
hierarchical planning, constraint-based reasoning

# FOREWORD

The paper presents a continuation of research and development reported in */Hess/*. The goal of this project consists in the development of a program for constructing source codes in a target language by interactive specifications where all dialogues are restricted to the field of application. Since the report */Hess/* was published, programs for target languages LAMBA, FORTRAN 77 and C were implemented with applications in medicine like analysis of microscopic slides or analysis of echocardiograms. In these applications, a PC-based image processing system from Data Translation was used. Also, for generating programs in dBase, the implementation of program construction rules for data base applications is under way. For these applications, special knowledge bases were generated. Based on these experiences, the concept of knowledge-based program construction was remodeled, and will be described in this report.

This system for knowledge based program construction is part of a general research program of implementation of an environment for the design and application of expert systems. This environment, *EXPERT Common Tools*, is implemented in Common LISP */Krie,Stee/* and its object-oriented extension */Bobr/*, and program construction and CAD are examples of application areas of this environment.

A rough scheme of the general architecture of EXPERT Common Tools is given in fig.0-1. All the objects which are relevant within several approaches to knowledge based systems or areas of application are placed within the central component of the environment, the *Inference Machine*. Operators on the *Strategy Level* may be considered to be meta-operators of the *Method Level*, and operators on the method level are performing specific tasks on the knowledge base, or the data base.

The *Problem Space* and the *Construction Space* are

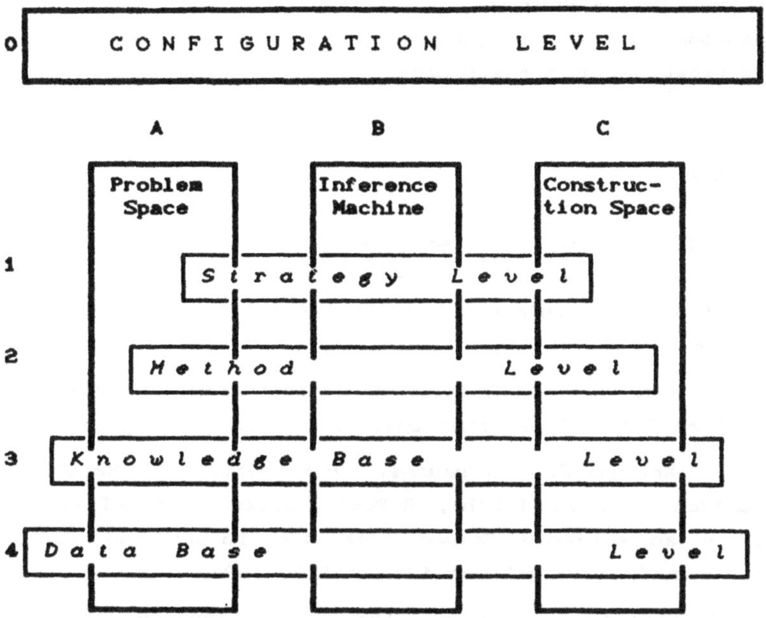


*Fig. 0-1: General architecture of the environment EXPERT Common Tools*

containing objects which are related to a specific area of application where the problem space is related to user-oriented interactions, and the construction space is related to automatic reasoning within the computer system.

By operators of the *Configuration Level* a special expert system may be configured by inserting appropriate operators into certain levels of the hierarchy.

In the paper it is shown how a specific expert system approach to knowledge based program construction fits into this general architecture. The different boxes in fig. 0-1 are indexed by 0 (configuration level), A1, B1, C1 (strategy level), A2, B2, C2 (method level), A3, B3, C3 (knowledge base level), and A4, B4, C4 (data base level).

This paper represents a status report, and besides well-established parts of the project supported by our previous implementations, e.g., there are many open questions within the possible conceptual extensions and specifications of our approach.

## References

/*Bobr*/ Bobrow,D.G., L.G.DeMichiel, R.P.Gabriel, S.E.Keene, G.Kiczales, D.A.Moon, Common LISP Object System Specification, Stanford University, X3J13 Document 88-002R, June 1988.

/*Hess*/ Hesse,R., R.Klette, Wissensbasierte Programmkonstruktion (1). ZKI Informationen, 3/87, Berlin, August 1987.

/*Krie*/ Kriegel,E., V.Bauche, H.Friedrich, W.Heicking, H.Jarosch, D.Koch, I.Mohr, R.Rosenmueller , EXPERT Common LISP - an extended Common LISP for 16-bit and 32-bit computers, Report, ZKI der ADW der DDR, 1988.

/*Stee*/ Steele,G., Common LISP: The Language. Digital Equipment Corporation, 1984.

## CONTENTS

*1. Knowledge based approach to program construction*

In approaches to automatic program synthesis, problems of the kinds as "Sort a list of n integers", "Find the maximum element of such a list" or "Solve the n-queens problem" are typically used for demonstrating logic-based, formalized design systems. For such a complexity level of computational problems, automatic solutions to program synthesis could be demonstrated already, e.g. */Man1,Man2,Man3,Fran/*. But in real world programming problems, the input are more complex processes or data structures and models for classes of processes or data are only characterizing these items at a certain level of abstraction. Here we are concerned with computational problems with a-priori data specifications by the user characterized by approximations, incompleteness, contradictions etc. Some of the remaining specifications of the programming task may be performed by automatic reasoning about operands and operators of the application area, and some have to be based on interactions with the human user and will not be automated in the next coming years according to the *state of the art* of knowledge based approaches and the complexity of the real world. For this cooperation of automatic and interactive specifications, we prefer to use the term *program construction* instead of *program synthesis* where the latter is basically restricted to automatic reasoning. The general structure of a program construction system which may be derived from our approach is shown in fig.1-1.

The *problem space* contains a model of the task to be solved by the program which has to be constructed. This model is formulated in terms of the domain of application and is stored within the domain specific *data base*. The *data base manager* acquires information from the domain oriented user considering semantic interdependencies of problem space terms and domain specific user behavior to answer requests scheduled by the *inference machine*.

The actual program construction process takes place

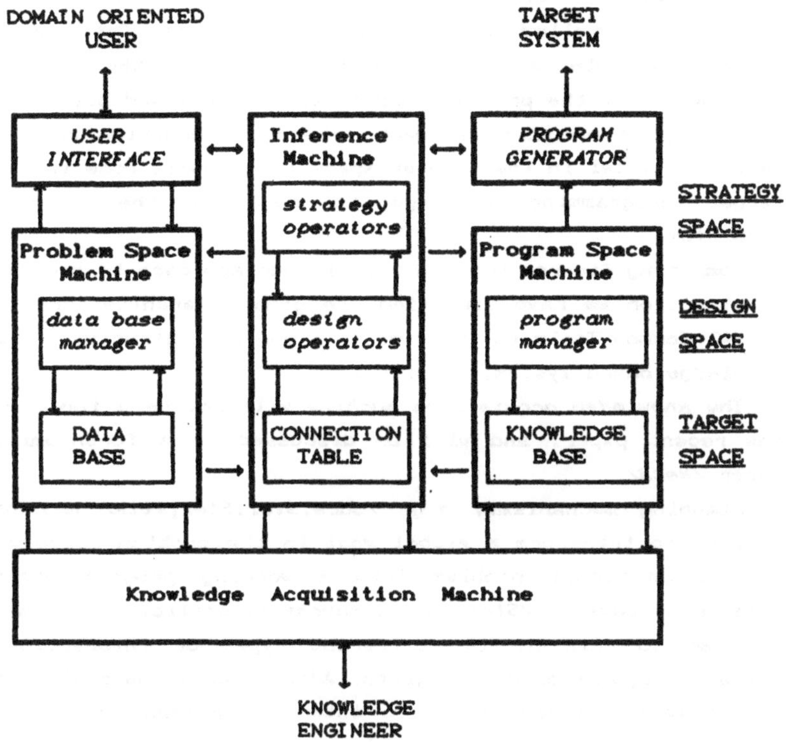


*Fig. 1-1: General structure of a knowledge based program construction system*

within the *program space* which is based on a specific domain independent language representing programming rules and partially specified programs. During this process, a diversity of possible hierarchical connections of rules of the domain specific *knowledge base* will be stepwise restricted to a unique characterization of a program. This restrictive process consists of repeated operations of refinement and specification.

The *connection table* specifies cross relations between program space and problem space. The program construction process and the interaction between program and problem space is controlled by the *inference machine*. Data base, connection table, and knowledge base determine the area of application of the program construction system and build the *target space* of this approach. The transformation of the generated model in the program space into source code in the target programming language is done by the *program generator*.

Comparing figures 0-1 and 1-1, in our approach to program construction we have specified the general architecture of EXPERT Common Tools to the case of a specific structure of a knowledge based system, see fig.1-2.

The *knowledge acquisition machine* will not be a topic of the recent paper, and will be discussed in a forthcoming paper */Hes3/*.

Planning mechanisms, e.g. */Sace,Ste1,Ste2,Wilk/* may be applied to transform a *global goal* in the problem space as the computational problem into a working program where *constraint posting /Ste1/* or *hierarchical control /Ste2/* may be used to maintain two different types of interactions between subgoals or data objects. Additionally, we shall use *reasoning on preconditions* to interact between activities within the program and the problem space.

A central problem of knowledge-based system design is posed by the request of implementing certain general models about the behaviour of the user in a specific area of application, and about the behaviour of the computer during program construction. For example, interactive specifications should be scheduled at the user interface by semantic complexes according to the point of view of the human user, and automatic specifications may be scheduled in the order as needed during program construction. This is an example of two cooperating models of the human user and of the program construction process which should be taken into account for scheduling the design steps of the program construction system. Following */Ste2/*, such guidance may be implemented by specific formulations of *strategy operators*

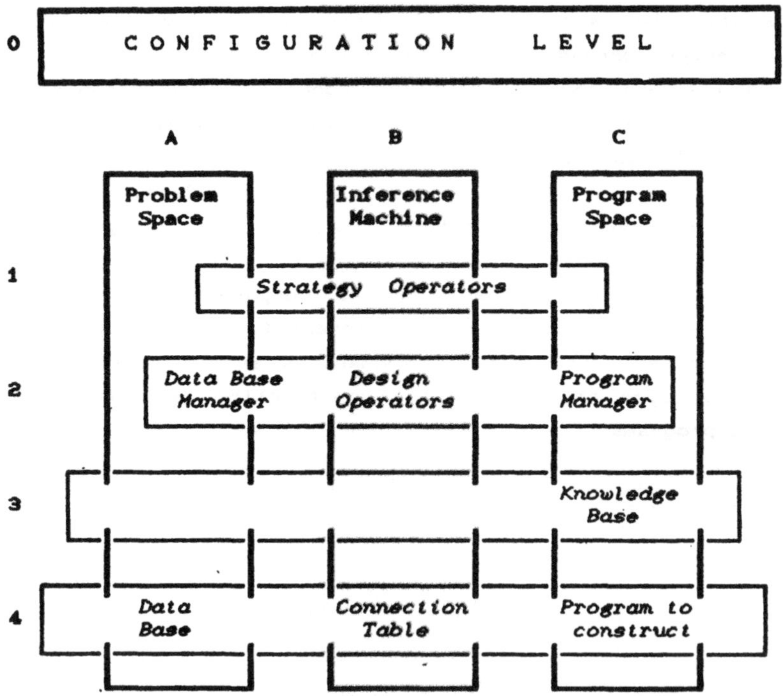


*Fig. 1-2: Unique specification of the program construction system within the EXPERT Common Tools architecture. The program generator may be considered to be a concrete operator of the program manager. By this figure it is suggested that further extensions of the approach are possible (A3, B3).*

communicating with the design space.

The *strategy space* as a whole is summerizing the meta-knowledge to select and schedule operators and operands of the design space to define a specific program construction system.

The *design space* represents the potential program

construction techniques. It contains *design operators* for specification and refinement during program construction, and *design operands* to control such a process.

The *target space* consists of operators and operands of the area of application where program construction has to be performed, as, e.g., analysis of microscopic slides in biomedicine, a flexible data base interface, or the interpretation of certain types of images in echocardiography.

The presented approach may be compared with that in */Krag/* where a programming environment for concurrent PEARL is described. Here, similar mechanisms as discussed in the present paper are applied for constructing "sceletons" of PEARL programs.

## 1.1. Denotations

In this paper, *syntactic categories* will be defined by using *context free grammars /Hopc/*. A grammar $\mathbb{G}=(\mathbb{N},\mathbb{T},\mathbb{P},S)$ consists of a set $\mathbb{N}$ of nonterminal symbols or variables, a set $\mathbb{T}$ of terminal symbols, a set $\mathbb{P}$ of productions, and a start symbol $S\in\mathbb{N}$. By $\mathbb{L}(\mathbb{G})$, the language generated by the grammar $\mathbb{G}$ is denoted.

We are using the conventions that symbols printed in *italics* denote the *terminals* of $\mathbb{T}$, bold printed symbols represent the *nonterminals* of $\mathbb{N}$, and CAPITALS represent attributes, relations or functions.

Each $\mathbf{N}\in\mathbb{N}$ is defining a syntactic category $\mathbb{L}(\mathbb{G}_N)$ by assuming $\mathbf{N}$ to be the start symbol of the (modified) grammar $\mathbb{G}_N=(\mathbb{N},\mathbb{T},\mathbb{P},\mathbf{N})$. $\mathbb{V}=\mathbb{N}\cup\mathbb{T}$ is called the *vocabulary* of grammar $\mathbb{G}$ and consists of *symbols*. The free monoid $\mathbb{V}^*=\mathbb{V}^+\cup\{\varepsilon\}$ consists of *words*, where $\varepsilon$ denotes the *empty word*. It holds that $\mathbb{L}(\mathbb{G})\subseteq\mathbb{T}^*$

For the evaluation of words $w_1,w_2,w_3,\ldots$ of the set $\mathbb{V}^*$, *attributes* $ATT_1,ATT_2,ATT_3,\ldots$ may be introduced. In general, such an attribute is a partial function on $\mathbb{V}^*$ mapping into a certain range of evaluation values. For example, the attribute LENGTH is defined on all words of $\mathbb{V}^*$ and mapping into the set of natural numbers, but a special instance of an attribute variable **semantic_interpretation** may be only defined on certain words in $\mathbb{T}^*$, mapping into a set of area-oriented structures.

For $x\in\mathbb{V}$ let $\mathbb{A}(x)$ be the set of attributes defined on symbol x. For example, for a terminal symbol *operator_type* assume $\mathbb{A}$(*operator_type*) = {COMPLEXITY,SUBTYPE}. For refering to attribute ATT of a symbol x we write x.ATT. For example, *operator_type*.COMPLEXITY denotes a certain value.

Let $p\in\mathbb{P}$ be a production. For symbols appearing in p, *attributation rules* are specifying methods to compute attributes of theses symbols. Let $\mathbb{R}(p)$ be the set of attributation rules for rule p. If a symbol appears several times in p then its different appearences are made distinctive by indexing. For example, the rule

$p_{selection}$ = selection ⟶ *then* statement *else* statement

is transformed into

$p_{selection}$ = selection ⟶ *then* $statement_1$ *else* $statement_2$,

and the set $\mathbb{R}(p_{selection})$ contains the attributation rule

selection.COMPLEXITY ← $k_{selection}$ * ($statement_1$.COMPLEXITY + $statement_2$.COMPLEXITY).

Besides the attributation rules $\mathbb{R}(p)$, sets $\mathbb{C}(p)$ may be defined to contain certain *attributation conditions* of production or rule p /*Goet*/. These conditions are logical expressions which must be satisfied on the set of attributes of the symbols contained in p. We shall use such sets $\mathbb{C}(p)$, formulated for conditions in the problem space, via the connection table correspondence for program construction rules, but in this paper not for productions of grammars.

For the calculation and the assignment of attributes to words of a language $\mathbb{L}(\mathbb{G})$ we consider a given grammar $\mathbb{G}=(\mathbb{N},\mathbb{T},\mathbb{P},\mathbb{S})$ to be part of an *attributed grammar* $\mathbb{AG}=(\mathbb{G},\mathbb{A},\mathbb{R},\mathbb{C})$ /*Goet*/ with

$$\mathbb{A} = \bigcup_{x\in\mathbb{V}} \mathbb{A}(x),$$

$$\mathbb{R} = \bigcup_{p\in\mathbb{P}} \mathbb{R}(p), \text{and}$$

$$\mathbb{C} = \bigcup_{p\in\mathbb{P}} \mathbb{C}(p).$$

In this paper, the attribute symbol $\chi$ is used as abbreviation of the attribute COMPLEXITY with the fixed interpretation to be a complexity measure of program space objects, and we do <u>not</u> claim that

$$\mathbb{A}(x)\cap\mathbb{A}(y)\neq\emptyset \rightarrow x=y$$

as in /*Goet*/. Identical attributes may be defined on different symbols. For example, in the sense of the present paper $\mathbb{AG}=((\mathbb{N},\mathbb{T},\mathbb{P},\mathbb{S}),\langle\chi\rangle,\mathbb{R})$ is an example of an attributed grammar without attributation conditions.

On sets of words several relations will be introduced in this report. A relation R defined on a set $\mathbb{A}$, i.e. $R\subseteq\mathbb{A}\times\mathbb{A}$, is called to be *irreflexive* iff (read: "if and only if")

$$\forall a(a\in\mathbb{A} \rightarrow \neg(aRa)),$$

to be *reflexive* iff

$$\forall a(a\in\mathbb{A} \rightarrow aRa),$$

to be *asymmetric* iff

$$\forall a\forall b(a\in\mathbb{A} \wedge b\in\mathbb{A} \wedge aRb \rightarrow \neg(bRa)),$$

to be *symmetric* iff

$$\forall a\forall b(a\in\mathbb{A} \wedge b\in\mathbb{A} \wedge aRb \rightarrow bRa),$$

and to be *transitive* iff

$$\forall a\forall b\forall c(a\in\mathbb{A} \wedge b\in\mathbb{A} \wedge c\in\mathbb{A} \wedge aRb \wedge bRc \rightarrow aRc).$$

For functions F and G we shall use $FG(\alpha)$ as abbreviation of the sequential application $F(G(\alpha))$ of these functions. Note that $FG\neq GF$ in general. Furthermore, we shall use $[FG](\alpha)$ as abbreviation of the parallel and independent application of the functions F and G on argument $\alpha$, if such an application is defined. Note that $[FG]=[GF]$.

For example, let $\alpha$ be a word of a language $\mathbb{L}$ defined on set $\mathbb{T}=\{0,1\}$, and let F be the replacement of all *0*'s by the string *0101*, and G be the replacement of all *1*'s by the string *1001*. Then $[FG](\alpha)$ is defined, and, e.g., it holds that $[FG](0110)=1001010101011001 \neq FG(0110)=F(0100110010)=$ *0101101010101110101010110101*.

With the marker ▮ we shall denote the end of an example or the end of a proof.

## 1.2 Example Discourse Area

For illustration of our approach throughout the paper we shall use examples from the application area of cardiology, where program construction is very suitable for creating programs. Here, the users of the construction system are physicians or other medical staff. By interactive dialogues, programs are to be constructed for interpreting specific types of cardiologic images, for producing different kinds of output.

An example discourse area within Cardiology is given by the generation of programs for *wall motion analysis* of silhouettes of the human heart. During systolic ejection, the left ventricular contraction may be classified to be *normal* if all points along the ventricular inner surface are performing a uniform cocentric inward motion. Such a coordinated contraction is called *synergy*. Abnormal patterns (*asynergy*) as disrupted or uncoordinated ventricular contraction are classified as *Akinesis*, *Asyneresis*, *Asynchrony*, *Dyskinesis*, or *Hypokinesis*.

A variety of methods for qualitative or quantitative evaluation of two-dimensional echocardiograms has been proposed in the medical literature. Because no standard of wall motion has been available, there is no objective evaluation of these methods. For example, the method illustrated in fig.1-3 is based on the assumption that calculated centers of the different silhouettes may be used for performing a superposition of these silhouettes. These silhouettes are traced manually, and certain types of *centers* and *main axis* are computed for this superpositioning.

By these remarks, a brief picture should be drawn to recognize the importance of flexible construction of programs in this area. By selecting a special approach to wall motion analysis, the general "architecture" of the program may be influenced as well as many "details" within this program. Then, this program allows operational work based on the selected approach.

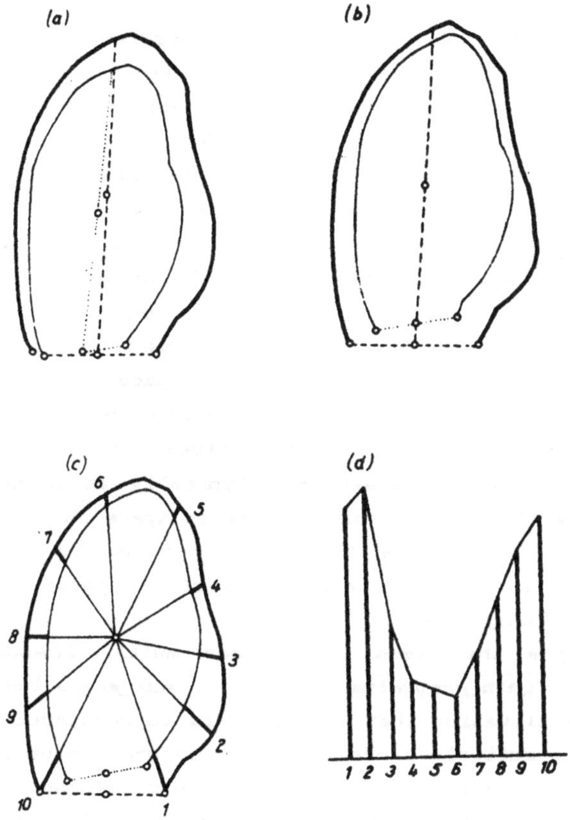


*Fig. 1-3: Demonstration of a special approach for analysing echocardiograms: Motion from enddiastole to endsystole may be evaluated, e.g., by*

*(a) shifting silhouettes into one position,*

*(b) superpositioning of both silhouettes,*

*(c) generating radiants, and*

*(d) calculating histograms of features based on these radiants*

*2. The Problem Space*

For an adequate represention of the problem which is to be solved by the constructed program, a representation tool is required to describe programming problems in terms of the application areas. This tool must be formal enough to meet the requirements of symbolic reasoning but also it must be comprehensive to the domain oriented user. Further it should include properties which allow the structuring of data base terms to semantic complexes to avoid permanent jumping between different points of view during user interaction. These requirements can be met by implementing a general relational representation of the problem space.

From the point of view of the inference machine each data base term consists of a pair (**key value**), where **key** is a variable which may be evaluated (typically as a string) within a semantic category of the problem space and **value** is a variable (which may be evaluated by values within the range of **key**) for a concrete instance of it specifying the actual programming task.

For example the items (*run_number mult*), (*image_type greyvalued*), (*min_greyvalue 0*) and (*max_greyvalue 63*) describe the situation that a program is to construct which is to perform multiple processing runs on grey value images with greyvalues ranging from 0 to 63. The data base manager of the problem space has to answer requests of the inference machine receiving the key-symbol and sending back the actual value.

To come up to all requirements above mentioned the *problem space representation* is used as shown in fig 2-1, CAPITALS indicate relation types.

Here, the variable semantic_group specifies a group of problem space items which belong together semantically and should be requested all together from the user or other sources of problem information at the moment if one of its keys is invoked by the inference machine. The relations RANGE, DEFAULT, REQUEST_TYPE and REQUEST determine a

```
(key (BELONGS_TO semantic_group)
     (SCOPE scope)
     (VALUE value)
     (RANGE range)
     (DEFAULT default_value)
     (REQUEST_TYPE request_type)
     (REQUEST request))
```

*Fig 2-1: Object structure as used for problem space items*

retrieval procedure which is processed by the data base manager in case of a data base request by the inference machine if the VALUE-slot has not yet been filled. To specifv the source of problem space information request_type may have different values, e.g. *user_request* or *automatic_request*.

In case of (REQUEST_TYPE *user_request*), the value of request points to a certain *communication data structure (CDS)* which will be send to the user interface to get the information directly from the user. The CDS also describes the mapping of the user answer into the set of valid values for key determined by range. Here, it is assumed that any value in range is consistent with the actual state of the construction system. The complex situation of the existence of interrelations between ranges of problem space terms may be represented by *constraints*, and mechanisms of constraint satisfaction have to be implemented in this case.

Otherwise, in case of request_type is equal to *automatic_request*, the value of request points to a *demon* which calculates the requested value automatically and returns it to the data base. Also the special symbols *default* and *unknown* may be returned in case of information retrieval. The value *default* causes the data base manager to copy the value of default_value into the value-slot. If the value-slot is set to *unknown* then the fact is indicated that further data base requests do not try again to retrieve the problem space information of key.

*automatic value retrieval:*

```
(min_grayvalue (BELONGS_TO image_features)
      (SCOPE permanent)
      (VALUE ?)
      (RANGE 0..255)
      (DEFAULT 0)
      (REQUEST_TYPE automatic_request)
      (REQUEST calc_min_grayval))
```

*interactive value retrieval:*

```
(output_device (BELONGS_TO result_output)
      (SCOPE temporary)
      (VALUE ?)
      (RANGE [display printer disk tape])
      (DEFAULT display)
      (REQUEST_TYPE user_request)
      (REQUEST output_device_menu)).
```

*Fig. 2-2: Examples of data base terms of the problem space.*

The slot SCOPE specifies the scope of validity of the data base term, i.e. in case of (SCOPE *permanent*) the VALUE-slot will remain unchanged after getting any value and in case of (SCOPE *temporary*) the VALUE-slot will be reset to 'unfilled' after a data base request by the inference machine. In such a way it becomes possible to distinguish between global and local problem space specifications.

By writing key.SLOT we are refering to the value of the slot SLOT of the data base term key.

In fig.2-2 there is an example of a data base term of the problem space where its value will be retrieved automatically. The demon *calc_min_grayval* is a procedure which calculates the minimum grayvalue from an image.

The next example in fig.2-2 is a data base term where its value is retrieved by user request.

A CDS may describe diffent types of user-system interactions like

*menu* - every menu exit is dedicated to one element of range, or

*parameter request* - the answer may be a valid numerical value or string within range.

The user controlled invocation of *help utilities* may also be

*CDS of menu type:*

```
(output_device_menu
   (TYPE menu)
   (HEADER 'Where are the results of the program
            to be sent to?')
   (EXITS (DISPLAY 'to the terminal display')
          (PRINTER 'to the laser printer')
          (DISK    'to a file of the default directory')
          (TAPE    'to a magnetic tape casette'))
   (HELP 'If you choose the display then no archivation
          of the program results is possible.'))
```

*CDS of parameter-request type:*

```
(number_of_images_request
   (TYPE parameter_request)
   (TEXT 'What is the number of images during a single
          investigation?')
   (HELP  nil))
```

*Fig. 2-3: Two examples of Communication Data Structures (CDS's).*

included into the CDS. The two examples in fig 2-3 show a CDS of menu type and a CDS of parameter-request type.

The given problem space representation as described by fig. 2-1 is a proposal and may be replaced by comfortable data base management systems, e.g. with natural language interaction, unless the interface to the inference machine will be injured.

*Conditions of the problem space* are syntactically represented by words of a formal context free language $\mathbb{L}_P(\mathbb{G}_P)$ generated by the grammar $\mathbb{G}_P(\mathbb{N}_P, \mathbb{T}_P, \mathbb{P}_P, \mathbf{condition})$, where subscript P indicates preconditions.

| | | |
|---|---|---|
| **condition** | ⟶ | *true* \| **predicate** \| **conjunction** \| **disjunction** \| **negation** |
| **conjunction** | ⟶ | *and* ( **condition condition** ) |
| **disjunction** | ⟶ | *or* ( **condition condition** ) |
| **negation** | ⟶ | *not* ( **condition** ) |
| **predicate** | ⟶ | ( **key** $\mathbf{relation}_{\mathbf{key}}$ $\mathbf{value}_{\mathbf{key}}$ ) |
| **key** | ⟶ | $\langle k \in \mathbb{K} \rangle$ |
| $\mathbf{value}_{\mathbf{key}}$ | ⟶ | $\langle v \in \mathbb{V}_{\mathbf{key}} \rangle$ |
| $\mathbf{relation}_{\mathbf{key}}$ | ⟶ | $\langle r \in \mathbb{R}_{\mathbf{key}} \rangle$ |

*Fig. 2-4: Productions of the grammar* $\mathbb{G}_P(\mathbb{N}_P, \mathbb{T}_P, \mathbb{P}_P, \mathbf{condition})$.

Using the conventions that symbols printed in *italics* denote the *terminals* of $\mathbb{T}_P$, bold printed symbols represent the nonterminals of $\mathbb{N}_P$ and expressions of the kind $\langle cond(a) \rangle$ are defining alternatives of all symbols a of $\mathbb{N}_P$ or $\mathbb{T}_P$ satisfying the unary relation *cond*, the productions of $\mathbb{P}_P$ determine $\mathbb{G}_P$ uniquely, where the start symbol is assumed to be the symbol **condition** $\in \mathbb{N}_P$. See fig. 2-4.

$\mathbb{K}$ is a set of problem space keys, $\mathbb{V}_{\mathbf{key}}$ is the set of problem space values with respect to a certain key **key**, and the set $\mathbb{R}_{\mathbf{key}}$ contains binary relations which are defined onto the set $\mathbb{V}_{\mathbf{key}} \times \mathbb{V}_{\mathbf{key}}$ of a certain key **key**. These keys and binary relations posses fixed interpretations within the field of application of the program construction system and may be used as range values for semantic interpretations. An expression

$$(\text{key relation}_{\text{key}}\ \text{value}_{\text{key}})$$

means that key.*value* $\text{relation}_{\text{key}}$ $\text{value}_{\text{key}}$ holds with respect to these fixed interpretations, where key.*value* is the actual value of the key key.

Three examples of problem space conditions are given in fig. 2-5 for illustration.

```
(a)   (min_grayvalue > 10)

(b)   and(
          (result_representation = graphical)
          (output_device = printer)
         )

(c)   and(
          or(
             not(
                  (sensor_view = LAO)
                 )
             (number_of_silhouettes > 2)
            )
          (volume_calculation_method = cylinder_slices)
         )
```

*Fig. 2-5: Examples of problem space conditions*
*(a) atomic condition*
*(b),(c) combined conditions*

### 3. *The Program Space*

Within the program space the hierarchical construction of programs takes place. Therefore, a representation of the actual state of the *design object*, i.e. of a partially specified program, is required as well as a representation of *construction steps*. The latter is the formal language of the knowledge base of the program space.

This knowledge base is a special implementation of operands and operators of the application field of the program construction system, and of relations between these operands and operators. It contains *rules* which describe decompositions of classes of program operators and operands, and these rules are used by refinement operators of the design space.

There are two classes of rules. The left hand side of an *operator refinement rule* describes a program operator more or less specified by a certain *operator domain* refering to certain operands as arguments, the right hand side contains a structure being considered as a refinement of the left hand side with operators and/or operands at a lower level of complexity. For the case of an *operand refinement rule*, left hand side and right hand side are characterized by *operand domains* defining operands at certain levels of complexity.

Relations between left hand and right hand side or binding limitations are expressed in form of *constraints* belonging to the rule.

Design objects created within the program space may be mapped by a *program generator* P GEN into the selected programming language of the target computer system. This modul P_GEN may be considered as performing a special *interpretation* of program space objects, given in an abstract program scheme language, within a common programming language.

### *3.1 Program Schemes*

*Program schemes* are words in an abstract *program scheme language* which defines a formal description of the design objects, i.e. of the actual programs constructed so far. Roughly, a program scheme may be characterized to be a collection of partially specified operators and operands which are linked by control and data flow relations, and between which certain dependencies are specified by constraints.

To define this language for representing program schemes first of all we have to consider some basic sets of terminal symbols such that the terminal alphabet of the language includes these sets. These sets may be considered to be 'universal' in the sense that any language for representing program schemes should be based on these sets.

But, the syntactic structure of program schemes as specified throughout this Section should be considered to be an example of a language which may be used in our approach. By replacing the grammar of program schemes the program generator P_GEN has to be modified in the approbriate way. Thus, this grammar specifies which type of target languages should be dealt with by the program generator most efficiently. Here, we are directed to procedural programming languages as Pascal, C, FORTRAN, e.g., as target languages.

### 3.1.1. *Hierarchies of operator and operand domains*

Let $\mathbb{F}$ be a finite set of program space *operator descriptors* ("$\mathbb{F}$" from function). For example, $\mathbb{F}$ = {*process_silhouettes*, *process_image*, *draw*, *approximate*, *print*, ...}.

$\Phi$ represents a partially ordered finite set of program space *operator domain symbols* where the ordering is interpreted by different levels of specification of operators. A transitive, asymmetric and irreflexive relation $\ll$ orders the elements $\phi \in \Phi$ within a *specialization tree* $(\Phi, \ll)$. The elements *opt_domain* of $\Phi$ are considered to be interpreted by objects

$$\text{opt\_domain} = \Xi(\textit{opt\_domain}),$$

e.g. an element $\textit{split} \in \Phi$ by a function $\text{SPLIT} = \Xi(\textit{split})$ which maps a data item into two data items according to a certain separation rule. The interpretation $\Xi$ is specific according to the field of application of the program construction system and is based on the fixed interpretations of the elements of sets $\mathbb{K}$, $\mathbb{R}_{key}$ and $\mathbb{V}_{key}$.

*Semantic interpretation* of relation $\ll$ on $\Phi$ :

> $\phi_i \ll \phi_j$ means that the function $\Xi(\phi_i)$ is a specialization of function $\Xi(\phi_j)$.

$\mathbb{X}_F$ is the set of *operator domain variables*. For example, $\mathbb{X}_F$={\$F1,\$F2,F22,F4,...}. Operators $f \in \mathbb{F}$ labeled by elements of $\mathbb{X}_F$ represent completely unspecified operators.

Operators $f \in \mathbb{F}$ of the program space labeled during program construction by leaves of the tree $(\Phi, \ll)$ are *terminal operators* with respect to further specifications. *Target operator domains* are labeling terminal operators which may be transformed by the program generator P_GEN into procedural constructs of the target programming language. Operators $f \in \mathbb{F}$ labeled during program construction by the root of $(\Phi, \ll)$ or by any $f \in \mathbb{X}_F$ are *most general operators* with respect to the construction process. Fig. 3.1-1 shows an

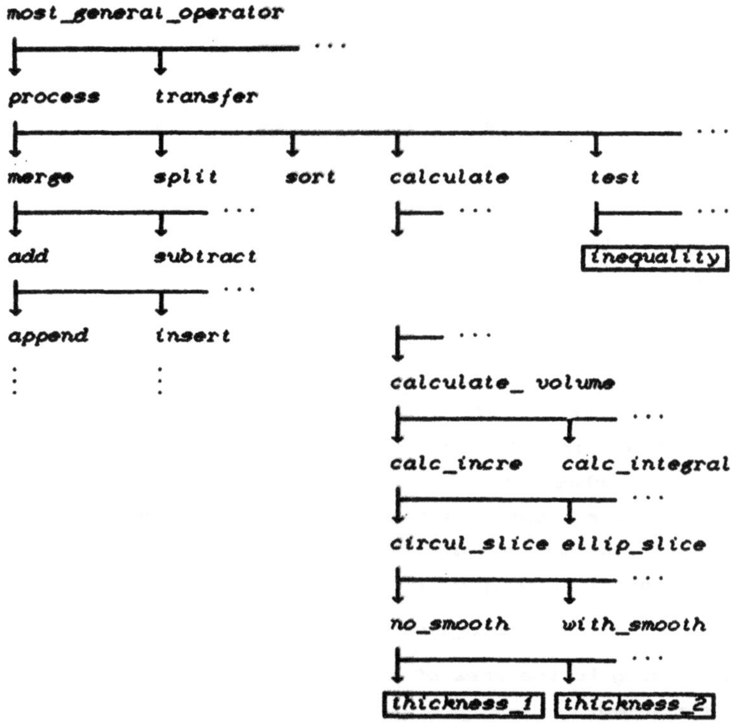


*Fig. 3.1-1: Example tree of a structure (Φ,<): $\phi \rightarrow \phi'$ means $\phi' \in$SUCC($\phi$). In the tree there are examples of common operator domains as well as examples of specific operator domains as used for specifying the calculation of the volume of the human heart in cardiology. Leaves of the tree are characterized by rectangles.*

example for a tree (Φ,<). Here, we have Φ = {*most_general_operator*, ..., *thickness_2*, ...}. Let $\phi_{root}$ be the root of the tree (Φ,<), i.e. $\phi_{root}$=*most_general_operator* in fig.3.1-1.

Let PRED($\phi$) be the *predecessor* of $\phi$ and SUCC($\phi$) be the set of *successors* of $\phi$ in tree (Φ,<), i.e.

$\phi' = \mathrm{PRED}(\phi) \leftrightarrow$

$$\phi \in \Phi \wedge \phi' \in \Phi \wedge \phi \ll \phi' \wedge \neg\exists\, \phi''(\phi'' \in \Phi \wedge \phi \ll \phi'' \wedge \phi'' \ll \phi')$$

$\phi' \in \mathrm{SUCC}(\phi) \leftrightarrow$

$$\phi \in \Phi \wedge \phi' \in \Phi \wedge \phi' \ll \phi \wedge \neg\exists\, \phi''(\phi'' \in \Phi \wedge \phi' \ll \phi'' \wedge \phi'' \ll \phi)$$

For any leaf node $\phi$ of the tree $(\Phi, \ll)$, the set $\mathrm{SUCC}(\phi)$ is empty, and the function PRED is not defined for $\phi_{root}$

Let $\mathbb{D}$ be the finite set of program space *operand descriptors* ("$\mathbb{D}$" from data). For example, $\mathbb{D}$ = {*echo_image*, *histogram*, *approximated silhouette*, *line*, *patient_data*, *heart_beat_rate*,...}.

$\Theta$ is a partially ordered finite set of program space *operand domain symbols* which may be used to determine the levels of specification of operands. Similarly to $(\Phi, \ll)$, also the elements $\theta \in \Theta$ are ordered as a *specialization tree* $(\Theta, \ll)$, i.e. the transitive, asymmetric and irreflexive specialization relation $\ll$ is extended from $\Phi$ to $\Theta$. Again, for element *opd_symbol*$\in\Theta$ a fixed interpretation

$$\text{opd\_symbol} = \mathfrak{I}(\textit{opd\_symbol})$$

according to the area of application of program construction is assumed.

*Semantic interpretation* of relation $\ll$ on $\Theta$ :

> $\theta_i \ll \theta_j$ means that data item $\mathfrak{I}(\theta_i)$ is more specific than data item $\mathfrak{I}(\theta_j)$.

$\mathcal{X}_D$ is the set of *operand domain variables*. For example $\mathcal{X}_D$={\$D1,\$D2,D22,D4,...}. Operands labeled by $d \in \mathcal{X}_D$ are completely unspecified operands.

Operands labeled during program construction by the leaves of the tree $(\Theta, \ll)$ are *terminal operands* with respect to further specifications. *Target operand domains* are labeling terminal operands which may be transformed by the program generator P_GEN onto data structures of the target programming language. *Most general operands* of a construction process are labeled by the root element $\theta_{root}$ of the tree $(\Theta, \ll)$ or by any $d \in \mathcal{X}_D$. One example for a tree

$(\Theta,\ll)$ is shown in Fig. 3.1-2. Here, we have

$$\Theta = \langle \textit{most\_general\_operand}, \ldots, \textit{rhomb\_nonfill} \rangle$$

and $\theta_{root}$=*most_general_operand*.

Let PRED($\theta$) be the *predecessor* of $\theta$ and SUCC($\theta$) be the set of *successors* of $\theta$ in tree $(\Theta,\ll)$, i.e.

$$\theta'=\mathrm{PRED}(\theta) \leftrightarrow$$
$$\theta\in\Theta \wedge \theta'\in\Theta \wedge \theta\ll\theta' \wedge\neg\exists\, \theta''(\theta''\in\Theta \wedge \theta\ll\theta'' \wedge \theta''\ll\theta')$$

$$\theta'\in\mathrm{SUCC}(\theta) \leftrightarrow$$
$$\theta\in\Theta \wedge \theta'\in\Theta \wedge \theta'\ll\theta \wedge\neg\exists\, \theta''(\theta''\in\Theta \wedge \theta'\ll\theta'' \wedge \theta''\ll\theta).$$

For any leaf node $\theta$ of the tree $(\Theta,\ll)$, the set SUCC($\theta$) is empty, and the function PRED is not defined for $\theta_{root}$.

*Definition 3.1-1 (Distance of specialization):* The *distance of specialization* DISP($z,z'$) of two operand or operator domains $z$ and $z'$ with

$$z'=z \text{ or } z'\ll z$$

will be defined to be the length of the (shortest) path from $z$ to $z'$ in the trees $(\Theta,\ll)$ or $(\Phi,\ll)$, respectively. The non-commutative function DISP is recursively defined by

(3.1-1.1) $\quad \mathrm{DISP}(\theta,\theta')=0 \;\leftrightarrow\; \theta\in\Theta \wedge \theta'\in\Theta \wedge \theta=\theta'$

(3.1-1.2) $\quad \mathrm{DISP}(\theta,\theta')=\mathrm{DISP}(\theta'',\theta')+1 \;\leftrightarrow\; \theta\in\Theta \wedge \theta'\in\Theta \wedge \theta''\in\mathrm{SUCC}(\theta) \wedge (\theta'\ll\theta'' \vee \theta'=\theta'')$

(3.1-1.3) $\quad \mathrm{DISP}(\phi,\phi')=0 \;\leftrightarrow\; \phi\in\Phi \wedge \phi'\in\Phi \wedge \phi=\phi'$

(3.1-1.4) $\quad \mathrm{DISP}(\phi,\phi')=\mathrm{DISP}(\phi'',\phi')+1 \;\leftrightarrow\; \phi\in\Phi \wedge \phi'\in\Phi \wedge \phi''\in\mathrm{SUCC}(\phi) \wedge (\phi'\ll\phi'' \vee \phi'=\phi'')$.

Taking into account that according to our interpretation the elements of the domain variable sets $\mathcal{X}_D$ and $\mathcal{X}_F$ are on the same level of specification like the roots $\theta_{root}$ and $\phi_{root}$ of the trees $(\Theta,\ll)$ and $(\Phi,\ll)$, respectively, the definition of DISP may be extended by

(3.1-2.1) $\quad \mathrm{DISP}(d,d')=0 \;\leftrightarrow\; d\in\mathcal{X}_D \wedge d'\in\mathcal{X}_D$

(3.1-2.2) $\quad \mathrm{DISP}(d,\theta)=\mathrm{DISP}(\theta_{root},\theta) \;\leftrightarrow\; d\in\mathcal{X}_D \wedge \theta\in\Theta$

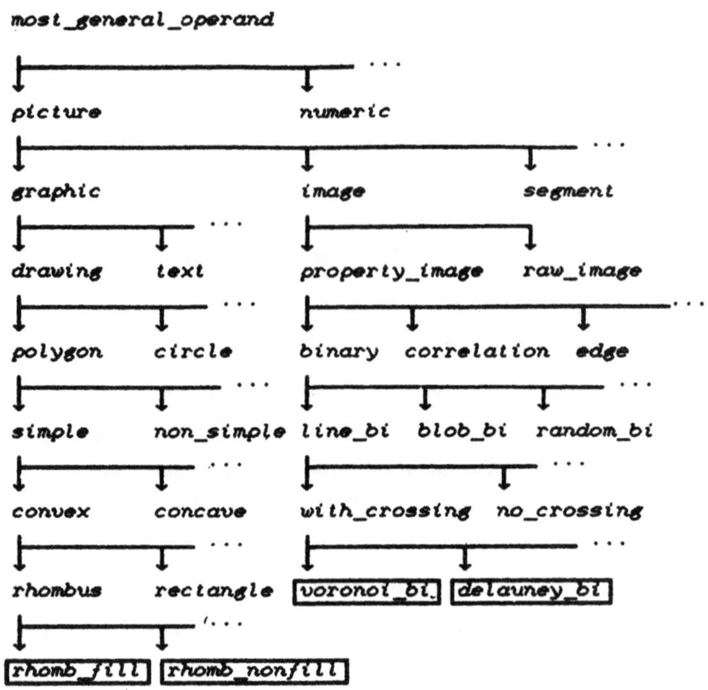


*Fig. 3.1-2: Example tree of a structure $(\Theta, \ll)$: $\theta \rightarrow \theta'$ means $\theta'$=SUCC($\theta$). In the tree there are examples of common operand domains as well as examples of specific operand domains as used for specifying image types in cardiology. Leaves of the tree are characterized by rectangles*

(3.1-2.3) $\quad DISP(f,f')=0 \qquad \leftrightarrow \quad f \in \mathcal{X}_F \wedge f' \in \mathcal{X}_F$

(3.1-2.4) $\quad DISP(f,\phi)=DISP(\phi_{root},\phi) \quad \leftrightarrow \quad f \in \mathcal{X}_F \wedge \phi \in \Phi$

On $\Theta$ and $\Phi$, the function DISP(z,z') is only defined for cases $z' \ll z$ or $z'=z$. To enable the calculation of negative distances of specialization we extend the definitions (3.1-1) and (3.1-2) by

(3.1-3.1) $\quad DISP(\theta,z')=-DISP(z',\theta) \quad \leftrightarrow$

$$\text{(3.1-3.2)}\quad \mathrm{DISP}(\phi,z')=-\mathrm{DISP}(z',\phi) \quad\leftrightarrow\quad \begin{array}{l} \theta\in\Theta \wedge ((z'\in\Theta \wedge \theta\ll z') \vee z'\in\mathcal{X}_D) \\ \phi\in\Phi \wedge ((z'\in\Phi \wedge \phi\ll z') \vee z'\in\mathcal{X}_F) \end{array}$$

Following this definition, in fig. 3.1-1, e.g., we have DISP(*calculate_volume*, *thickness_1*) = 4 and DISP(*inequality*, X) = -3, and in fig. 3.1-2 we have DISP(*rhomb_fill*, *polygon*) = -4 and DISP(Y, *voronoi_bi*) = 7. The values DISP(*no_smooth*, *ellip_slice*) or DISP(*graphic*, *image*) are not defined, for example.

Note that domain variables of sets $\mathcal{X}_F$ and $\mathcal{X}_D$ are printed bold, or, later on, in normal density with a preceeding '$'

The *sets of corresponding leaf nodes* of an operand domain $\theta$ or an operator domain $\phi$ are defined by

$$\mathbb{L}(\theta)=\{\theta' \mid \theta'\in\Theta \wedge (\theta'=\theta \vee \theta'\ll\theta) \wedge \neg\exists\theta''(\theta''\in\Theta \wedge \theta''\ll\theta')\}$$

and

$$\mathbb{L}(\phi)=\{\phi' \mid \phi'\in\Phi \wedge (\phi'=\phi \vee \phi'\ll\phi) \wedge \neg\exists\phi''(\phi''\in\Phi \wedge \phi''\ll\phi')\}.$$

For example, $\mathbb{L}$(*no_smooth*)={*thickness_1*, *thickness_2*, ...} in fig. 3.1-1, and $\mathbb{L}$(*graphic*)={*rhomb_fill*, *rhomb_nonfill*, ...} in fig. 3.1-2. Note that for any $\theta\in\Theta$ we have $\mathrm{card}(\mathbb{L}(\theta))>0$, and $\mathrm{card}(\mathbb{L}(\phi))>0$ for any $\phi\in\Phi$. For $\theta'\in\mathbb{L}(\theta)$, the function $\mathrm{DISP}(\theta,\theta')$ is always defined as well as $\mathrm{DISP}(\phi,\phi')$ for $\phi'\in\mathbb{L}(\phi)$. For any leaf node $z$ we have $\mathbb{L}(z)=\{z\}$.

For two domain symbols $z$ and $z'$ it holds that

$$z\ll z' \longrightarrow \mathbb{L}(z)\subseteq\mathbb{L}(z').$$

For evaluating the *complexity* of operand domains and operator domains quantitatively a *complexity measure* $\chi$ will be defined in the next Section.

### *3.1.2. Complexity of domain symbols*

A measure defined on the sets of domain symbols is called *monotone* iff (iff = "if and only if") for two domain symbols $z$ and $z'$ with $z \ll z'$ it holds that

$$\chi(z) < \chi(z'),$$

and it is called *balanced* iff there exists a constant $\varepsilon > 0$ such that for any domain symbol $z$ with the corresponding set $\mathbb{L}(z)$ of leaf nodes it holds that

$$|\chi(z) * \mathrm{card}(\mathbb{L}(z)) - \sum_{z' \in \mathbb{L}(z)} \mathrm{DISP}(z, z')| \leq \varepsilon,$$

where $\varepsilon$ is constant for measure $\chi$ on any tree of domain symbols.

A complexity measure is called *sound* iff it is monotone and balanced.

In the case of defining a measure $\chi$ by the maximum distance to the corresponding leaves,

$$\chi(z) = \max_{z' \in \mathbb{L}(z)} \mathrm{DISP}(z, z'),$$

this *maximum complexity measure* $\chi$ is monotone but not balanced.

In the case of taking the medium distance to the corresponding leaves,

$$\chi(z) = (1/\mathrm{card}\ \mathbb{L}(z)) \sum_{z' \in \mathbb{L}(z)} \mathrm{DISP}(z, z'),$$

this *medium complexity measure* $\chi$ is not monotone , see fig.3.1-3, but balanced with $\varepsilon = 0$.

We consider the investigation of different approaches to the calculation of appropriate complexity measures as an interesting problem for further research. Especially, the question should be answered whether there exists a sound measure or not.

But, more general, further experiments are necessary to evaluate different measures according to their relevance for

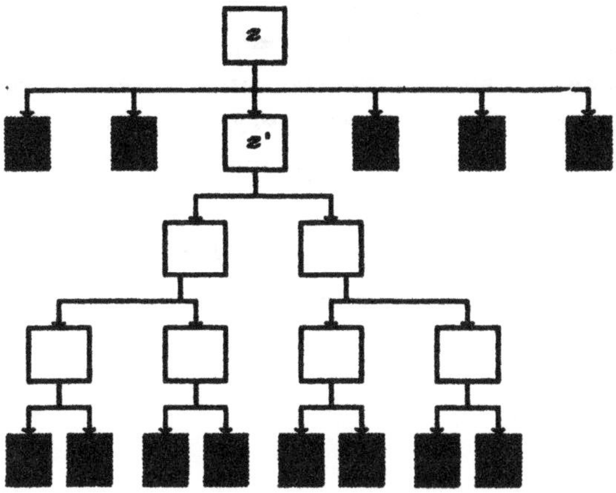


*Fig. 3.1-3: Example of a situation with $z' \in SUCC(z)$, but $\chi(z') > \chi(z)$ for the case of the medium complexity measure. Here, $\chi(z) = 37/13 = 2.8461...$ and $\chi(z') = 24/8 = 3$, i.e. z is evaluated as "more specified" in comparison to z'*

controlling the program construction process as discussed later on. If not otherwise specified, we shall use the medium complexity measure in our approach.

*Definition 3.1-2 (Domain complexity):* The *operand domain complexity* of an operand domain symbol $\theta$ or an operand domain variable $d \in \mathcal{X}_D$ is defined to be the medium distance of specialization to the leaves of its subtree or of tree $(\Theta, <)$ respectively Formally, a function $\chi$: $\Theta \cup \mathcal{X}_D \rightarrow \mathbb{N}_0$ is defined where $\mathbb{N}_0$ denotes the set of natural numbers,

$$(3.1\text{-}4.1) \quad \chi(\theta) = (1/\text{card}\ \mathbb{L}(\theta)) \sum_{\theta' \in \mathbb{L}(\theta)} \text{DISP}(\theta, \theta')$$

$$\leftrightarrow \quad \theta \in \Theta,$$

$$(3.1\text{-}4.2) \quad \chi(d) = \chi(\theta_{root})$$

$$\leftrightarrow \quad d \in \mathcal{X}_D .$$

*The operator domain complexity* of an operator domain symbol $\phi$ or an operator domain variable $f \in \mathcal{X}_F$ is defined to be the medium distance of specialization to the leaves of its subtree or of the tree $(\Phi, <)$ respectively. Formally, the function $\chi$ is extended by $\chi: \Phi \cup \mathcal{X}_F \longrightarrow \mathbb{N}_0$, and this extension is defined by

(3.1-5.1) $$\chi(\phi) = (1/\text{card}\,\mathbb{L}(\phi)) \sum_{\phi' \in \mathbb{L}(\phi)} \text{DISP}(\phi, \phi')$$

$$\leftrightarrow \quad \phi \in \Phi,$$

(3.1-5.2) $$\chi(f) = \chi(\phi_{root})$$

$$\leftrightarrow \quad f \in \mathcal{X}_F.$$

According to this definition, for any leaf node $z$ we have $\chi(z)=0$. For example, in fig. 3.1-1 we have $\chi$(*thickness_1*)=0, $\chi$(*calculate_volume*) =(1/n)*(4+4+...) with n≥2, and in fig. 3.1-2 we have $\chi$(*rhomb_fill*)=0.

### 3.1.3. *Syntactic definitions*

In Section 1.1 the basic notions for dealing with context free grammars and attributed grammars were given. In this Section, program schemes will be syntactically defined step by step, starting with the definition of the syntactic representation of operands (data items) and operators (functions) using the domain sets as terminal alphabets.

*Operands of the program space* are represented by words of a formal context free language $\mathbb{L}_D(\mathbb{G}_D)$ generated by the grammar $\mathbb{G}_D=(\mathbb{N}_D,\mathbb{T}_D,\mathbb{P}_D,\mathbf{operand})$ where subscript D indicates data. See fig.3.1-4, where the conventions are used that symbols printed with *italics* denote the terminals of $\mathbb{T}_D$, bold printed symbols represent the nonterminals of $\mathbb{N}_D$ and expressions of the kind <*cond*(*a*)> are defining an element *a* of $\mathbb{N}_D$ or $\mathbb{T}_D$ satisfying the unary relation *cond*. These productions of $\mathbb{P}_D$ determine $\mathbb{G}_D$, where the start symbol is assumed to be **operand**.

The attribute $\chi$ represents the complexity as initialized above in equations (3.1-4) and (3.1-5). The complexity of any operand

$$d(data\_type\_inst, data\_flow\_inst) \in \mathbb{L}_D(\mathbb{G}_D)$$

is expressed by

$$d.\chi$$

For any production $P_i$ in fig.3.1-4 there are one or two attributation rules in the set $\mathbb{R}(P_i)$.

The attribute $\nu$ of the syntactic category **data_type_list** was introduced to calculate the number of slots of a record data structure.

The syntactic category **data_flow** describes the data flow type of an operand. The *semantic interpretation* is straightforward:

> Operands labeled by data flow type *in* can only be read by operators, *out*-operands may be assigned values only and *inout* enables both reading and writing the operand value.

$P_1$: operand $\longrightarrow$ $\langle d \in \mathbb{D} \rangle$ ( data_type , data_flow )
$\mathbb{R}(P_1)$ = $\langle$operand.$\chi \leftarrow$ data_type.$\chi$ $\rangle$

$P_2$: data_flow $\longrightarrow$ *in* | *out* | *inout*
$\mathbb{R}(P_2)$ = $\langle\rangle$

$P_3$: data_type $\longrightarrow$ operand_domain
$\mathbb{R}(P_3)$ = $\langle$data_type.$\chi \leftarrow$ operand_domain.$\chi$ $\rangle$

$P_4$: data_type $\longrightarrow$ compound_type
$\mathbb{R}(P_4)$ = $\langle$data_type.$\chi \leftarrow$ compound_type.$\chi$ $\rangle$

$P_5$: operand_domain $\longrightarrow$ $\langle z \in (\Theta \cup \mathcal{X}_D) \rangle$
$\mathbb{R}(P_5)$ = $\langle$operand_domain.$\chi \leftarrow \chi(z)\rangle$

$P_6$: compound_type $\longrightarrow$ *vector* ( length , data_type )
$\mathbb{R}(P_6)$ = $\langle$compound_type.$\chi \leftarrow k_{vector} *$ data_type.$\chi$ $\rangle$

$P_7$: compound_type $\longrightarrow$ *list* ( data_type )
$\mathbb{R}(P_7)$ = $\langle$compound_type.$\chi \leftarrow k_{list} *$ data_type.$\chi$ $\rangle$

$P_8$: compound_type $\longrightarrow$ *record* ( data_type_list )
$\mathbb{R}(P_8)$ = $\langle$compound_type.$\chi \leftarrow k_{record} *$ (data_type_list.$\chi$ / data_type_list.$\nu$) $\rangle$

$P_9$: length $\longrightarrow$ ( $\langle n \in (\mathbb{N}_0 \cup \mathcal{X}_D) \rangle$ )
$\mathbb{R}(P_9)$ = $\langle\rangle$

$P_{10}$: data_type_list $\longrightarrow$ data_type
$\mathbb{R}(P_{10})$ = $\langle$data_type_list.$\chi \leftarrow$ data_type.$\chi$ , data_type_list.$\nu \leftarrow 1$ $\rangle$

$P_{11}$: data_type_list$_1$ $\longrightarrow$ data_type , data_type_list$_2$
$\mathbb{R}(P_{11})$ = $\langle$data_type_list$_1$.$\chi \leftarrow$ data_type.$\chi$ + data_type_list$_2$.$\chi$ , data_type_list$_1$.$\nu \leftarrow$ data_type_list$_2$.$\nu + 1$ $\rangle$

*Fig. 3.1-4: Productions of the grammar* $\mathbb{G}_D = (\mathbb{N}_D, \mathbb{T}_D, \mathbb{P}_D,$ operand$)$.

Operands which are only in the data flow relation *in* are refered to as *parameters*.

The nonterminal symbol data_type represents a more or

$P_{12}$: operator $\longrightarrow$ ⟨/def⟩ ( operator_type , [ ] )

$\mathbb{R}(P_{12})$= {operator.$\chi$ ← operator_type.$\chi$ ⟩

$P_{13}$: operator $\longrightarrow$ ⟨/def⟩ ( operator_type ,
[ operands ] )

$\mathbb{R}(P_{13})$= ⟨operator.$\chi$ ← operator_type.$\chi$ +
SIGN(operator_type.$\chi$)*$k_{op}$*(operands.$\chi$ / operands.$\nu$)⟩

$P_{14}$: operator_type $\longrightarrow$ operator_domain

$\mathbb{R}(P_{14})$= ⟨operator_type.$\chi$ ← operator_domain.$\chi$ ⟩

$P_{15}$: operands $\longrightarrow$ operand

$\mathbb{R}(P_{15})$= ⟨operands.$\chi$ ← operand.$\chi$ ,
operands.$\nu$ ← 1⟩

$P_{16}$: operands$_1$ $\longrightarrow$ operand , operands$_2$

$\mathbb{R}(P_{16})$= ⟨operands$_1$.$\chi$ ← operand.$\chi$ + operands$_2$.$\chi$ ,
operands$_1$.$\nu$ ← operands$_2$.$\nu$ + 1 ⟩

$P_{17}$: operator_domain $\longrightarrow$ ⟨z∈($\mathbb{S}\cup\mathbb{X}_F$)⟩

$\mathbb{R}(P_{17})$= ⟨operator_domain.$\chi$ ← $\chi$(z)⟩

*Fig. 3.1-5: Remaining productions of grammar*
$\mathbb{G}_F$=($\mathbb{N}_F$, $\mathbb{T}_F$, $\mathbb{P}_F$, operator).

less specific data type description which may be structured into different arrangements of subtypes like *vectors*, *lists*, or *records*, or may be a (scalar) operand_domain. Domains of operands or subdomains within data_type-structures may be characterized as *not yet defined* by evaluating them with a variable from $\mathbb{X}_D$ in place of operand_domain.

*Operators of the program space* may be represented by words of a formal context free language $\mathbb{L}_F(\mathbb{G}_F)$ generated by the grammar $\mathbb{G}_F$=($\mathbb{N}_F$, $\mathbb{T}_F$, $\mathbb{P}_F$, operator) with

$$\mathbb{T}_F \supset \mathbb{T}_D,\ \mathbb{N}_F \supset \mathbb{N}_D \text{ and } \mathbb{P}_F \supset \mathbb{P}_D.$$

Under the same conventions like above, in addition to $\mathbb{P}_D$ the productions of $\mathbb{P}_F$ as shown in fig. 3.1-5 do complete $\mathbb{G}_F$.

The nonterminal symbol operator_domain represents a more or less specific operator description which may be

$P_{18}$: program_scheme $\longrightarrow$ *begin end* .

$\mathbb{R}(P_{18})$= <program_scheme.$\chi \leftarrow 0$>

$P_{19}$: program_scheme $\longrightarrow$ *begin* statements *end* .

$\mathbb{R}(P_{19})$= <program_scheme.$\chi \leftarrow$ statements.$\chi$ >

$P_{20}$: statements $\longrightarrow$ statement

$\mathbb{R}(P_{20})$= <statements.$\chi \leftarrow$ statement.$\chi$ >

$P_{21}$: $\text{statements}_1$ $\longrightarrow$ statement ; $\text{statements}_2$

$\mathbb{R}(P_{21})$= <$\text{statements}_1.\chi \leftarrow$ statement.$\chi$ + $\text{statements}_2.\chi$ >

$P_{22}$: statement $\longrightarrow$ operator

$\mathbb{R}(P_{22})$= <statement.$\chi \leftarrow$ operator.$\chi$ >

$P_{23}$: operator_type $\longrightarrow$ program_scheme

$\mathbb{R}(P_{23})$= <operator_type.$\chi \leftarrow 0$ >

$P_{24}$: statement $\longrightarrow$ structure

$\mathbb{R}(P_{24})$= <statement.$\chi \leftarrow$ structure.$\chi$ >

$P_{25}$: structure $\longrightarrow$ *begin* statements *end*

$\mathbb{R}(P_{25})$= <structure.$\chi \leftarrow$ statement.$\chi$ >

$P_{26}$: structure $\longrightarrow$ *if* b_operand selection

$\mathbb{R}(P_{26})$= <structure.$\chi \leftarrow k_{if}$ + selection.$\chi$ >

$P_{27}$: structure $\longrightarrow$ repetition

$\mathbb{R}(P_{27})$= <structure.$\chi \leftarrow$ repetition.$\chi$ >

$P_{28}$: selection $\longrightarrow$ *then* statement

$\mathbb{R}(P_{28})$= <selection.$\chi \leftarrow k_{then} *$ statement.$\chi$ >

$P_{29}$: selection $\longrightarrow$ *then* $\text{statement}_1$ *else* $\text{statement}_2$

$\mathbb{R}(P_{29})$= <selection.$\chi \leftarrow k_{then\_else} *$($\text{statement}_1$ $\chi$+$\text{statement}_2.\chi$)>

$P_{30}$: repetition $\longrightarrow$ *while* b_operand *do* statement

$\mathbb{R}(P_{30})$= <repetition.$\chi \leftarrow k_{while} + k_{do} *$ statement.$\chi$ >

$P_{31}$: repetition$\longrightarrow$ *repeat* statements *until* b_operand

$\mathbb{R}(P_{31})$= <repetition.$\chi \leftarrow k_{repeat} + k_{until} *$ statements.$\chi$ >

$P_{32}$: b_operand $\longrightarrow$ <deD> ( *boolean* , *in* )

$\mathbb{R}(P_{32})$= <>

*Fig. 3.1-6: Remaining productions of grammar* $\mathbb{G}_S$.

characterized as *partially specified* according to the position of the operator domain $\phi$ within the specification tree $(\Phi,<)$, or as *unspecified* in case of evaluating it with a variable from $\mathbb{X}_F$.

The function SIGN(x) used in the definition of $\mathbb{R}(P_{13})$ is defined to be equal to 0 if x=0, and 1 otherwise.

Now complete *program schemes of the program space* may be represented by words of a formal context free language $\mathbb{L}_S(\mathbb{G}_S)$ generated by the extended grammar $\mathbb{G}_S(\mathbb{N}_S,\mathbb{T}_S,\mathbb{P}_S,$program_scheme) with

$$\mathbb{T}_S\supset\mathbb{T}_F,\ \mathbb{N}_S\supset\mathbb{N}_F \text{ and } \mathbb{P}_S\supset\mathbb{P}_F.$$

The productions of $\mathbb{P}_S$ shown in fig.3.1-6 do complete $\mathbb{G}_S$. Here we assume that *boolean*$\in\Phi$.

Now, in place of the category operator_type of grammar $\mathbb{G}_F=(\mathbb{N}_F,\mathbb{T}_F,\mathbb{P}_F,$operator), operators may be characterized by a complete instance of a program_scheme as the refinement structure of the operator. Note that for that reason, the nonterminal operator_type was introduced in grammar $\mathbb{G}_F$.

*Example 3.1-3:* Using the syntax of $\mathbb{L}_S$ an example program scheme may be represented by

```
begin
 set(set_const,[ans(boolean,out),
                val(true,in)]);
 while ans(boolean,in) do
  begin
   scan(tv_scan,[pict(image,out)]);
   process(image_proc,[pict(image,in),
                       res(m_g_operand,out)]);
   user_request($F1,[request(string,in),
                     ans(boolean,out)])
  end
end.
```

∎

The productions $\mathbb{P}_S$ describe the control flow within program structures consisting of cooperating operators which are linked by operands.

The program generator P_GEN is mapping such a program scheme into source code of the target language of the program construction system. Of course, because our language $\mathbb{L}_S(\mathbb{G}_S)$ is complete in the sense of the thesis of *Church* and *Turing* (i.e., it is of the same descriptive power as algorithmic languages based on, e.g. the Turing machine */Hopc/*), the program generator P_GEN may map into any programming language in principle, and may generate any program in this language in principle. But, because our productions $P_1, P_2, P_3, \ldots$ are oriented to imperative languages, the specified representation of program schemes is appropriate to languages as PASCAL, C, or FORTRAN. In the case that descriptive languages as LISP or PROLOG should be used as target language, the given grammar $\mathbb{G}_S$ should be modified to simplify the program generator P_GEN.

Program schemes are used to represent the refinement of operators and operands of the program space at different levels of refinement and relations between those refinement levels are relations between program schemes and their subschemes at subsequent levels of refinement, see production $P_{23}$.

Altogether these program schemes are hierarchically ordered and this hierarchy characterizes the actual state of the program which has to be designed.

Refinement operators of the design space are mapping operators of a given program scheme onto program schemes (CHILD *schemes*) which are informationally connected via common operands (GLOBAL *data*), see fig.3.1-7, or are mapping operands of a parent scheme onto operands (CHILD *operands*). The inverse relation (PARENT *scheme*) points backward.

The measure $\chi$ is a generalization of approaches to quantify the program complexity described by */Rech/*. The constants $k_{vector}, \ldots, k_{until}$ are selected as follows in our approach:

$k_{vector}=1.25$, $k_{list}=1.5$, $k_{record}=1.75$, $k_{op}=1.0$,

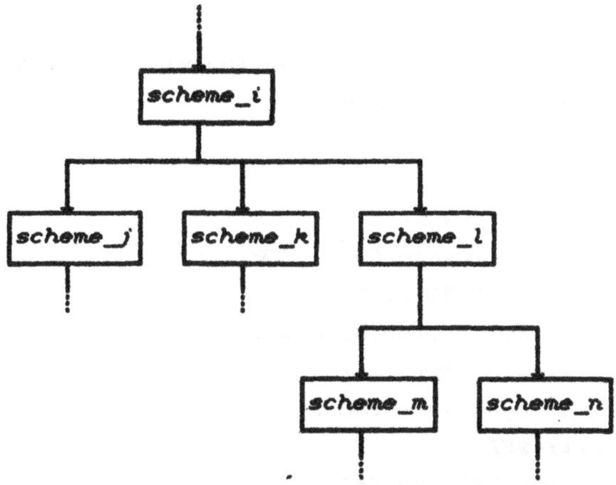


*Fig. 3.1-7: Within program scheme 'scheme_i' three operators were refined by program schemes 'scheme_j','scheme_k' and 'scheme_l'.*

$k_{if}$=2, $k_{then}$=1.5, $k_{then\_else}$=3, $k_{while}$=2,

$k_{do}$=1.5, $k_{repeat}$=2, $k_{until}$=1.5

based on subjective evaluations of examples.

*Example 3.1-4:* To illustrate this measure $\chi$, let us consider the algorithm of MERGESORT as known in combinatorical programming. Using the syntax of $\mathbb{L}_S$ a program scheme $P_{sort} \in \mathbb{L}_S$ for refining an operator *sort* is given in fig. 3.1-8.

Then, for the complexity $P_{sort}.\chi$ of this program scheme it holds that

$$P_{sort}.\chi = test.\chi + (if \ldots then \ldots).\chi$$
$$= (inequality.\chi + 0.75) +$$
$$2 + 1.5 * (separate.\chi + sort1.\chi + sort2.\chi + merge.\chi)$$

Note that $F1, $F2, $F3 are not yet specified, and their complexity value is $\chi(\phi_{root})=\chi(most\_general\_operator)$. ∎

```
begin
 test(inequality,[n(integer,in),n1(1,in),t(boolean,out)]);
 if t(boolean,in) then
  begin
   separate($F1,
     [length1($D11,in),
      array1(vector($D11,$D2),in),
      length2($D12,out),
      array2(vector($D12,$D2),out),
      length3($D13,out),
      array3(vector($D13,$D2),out)]);
   sort1($F2,
     [length2($D12,in),
      array2(vector($D12,$D2),in_out)]);
   sort2($F2,
     [length3($D13,in),
      array3(vector($D13,$D2),in_out)]);
   merge(append,
     [array1(vector($D11,$D2),out),
      length2($D12,in),
      array2(vector($D12,$D2),in),
      length3($D13,in),
      array3(vector($D13,$D2),in)])
  end
end.
```

*Fig. 3.1-8: Algorithm* MERGESORT *in the syntax of language* $\mathbb{L}_S$.

On the basis of these introductory definitions of syntactical categories, in the following sections several basic definitions for the application of operators and operands will be given which will further allow to discuss different ways to implement inference mechanisms within our approach to knowledge based program construction. These definitions may be considered to be the "core ideas" of the presented approach. In Appendix 1 an extensive example for deriving words in language $\mathbb{L}_S$ is given.

### 3.2 Matching and Unification of Operands

A program space operand was defined to be a word $d(d_t, d_f)$ of the language $\mathbb{L}_D$ , with $d \in \mathbb{D}$, $d_t$ and $d_f$ are in the syntactic categories data_type and data_flow respectively. For example,

*array_11(vector($D1,$D2),in_out)* or
*length_total(integer,in)*

are words of the language $\mathbb{L}_D$, i.e. program space operands, with

$d_t$ = *vector($D1,$D2)* and $d_f$ = *in_out*, or
$d_t$ = *integer* and $d_f$ = *in*,

respectively.

Because the descriptor $d \in \mathbb{D}$ is nothing else than a unique name of the given operand $d(d_t, d_f)$, in the following we shall say that operands $d(d_t, d_f)$ and $d'(d_t, d_f)$ are *isomorphic*. Furthermore, if $d_t$ and $d_t'$ are different just by different names of variables contained in both words, also the operands $d(d_t, d_f)$ and $d'(d_t', d_f)$ are *isomorphic*. But, non-identical variables may not be identified by such renamings, i.e. *vector($D1,$D2)* and *vector($D4,$D1)* are isomorphic, but *vector($D1,$D2)* and *vector($D6,$D6)* are not.

### *3.2.1 Specification of data types*

We shall extent the relation « which has been defined between elements of the set $\Phi$ of operator domain symbols and between elements of the set $\Theta$ of operand domain symbols. Now, also words of the syntactic category data_type of the grammar $\mathbb{G}_D$ defined in fig.3.1-4 have to be compared.

We introduce a relation ««« which may be interpreted to be a specification relation between words.

Let $\mathbb{DT}$ be the language generated by the modified grammar $(\mathbb{N}_D, \mathbb{T}_D, \mathbb{P}_D$, data_type), i.e. $\mathbb{DT}$ is the syntactic category data_type of the grammar $\mathbb{G}_D$ defined in fig.3.1-3.

For example,

*integer*, $D1, *vector(list(integer)*,$D2)

are words of the language $\mathbb{DT}$. Words of this language $\mathbb{DT}$ are called *isomorphic* if they are identical up to different variables $D1,D1,... appearing in these words, but without identifying different variables. For example, *vector(list(integer)*,$D2) and *vector(list(integer)*,D12) are isomorphic words of this language $\mathbb{DT}$.

*Definition 3.2-1 (Specification relation «««):* Two words $z_1$, $z_2$ of the language $\mathbb{DT}$ are in relation $z_1 ⋘ z_2$ iff one of the following cases holds:

(3.2-1.1) $z_1 \in \Theta \wedge z_2 \in \Theta \wedge z_1 \ll z_2$

(3.2-1.2) $z_2 \in \mathcal{X}_D$

(3.2-1.3) $z_1 = vector(\theta_1, z_1') \wedge z_2 = vector(\theta_2, z_2') \wedge$
$(\theta_1 \ll \theta_2 \wedge z_1' = z_2') \vee (\theta_1 = \theta_2 \wedge z_1' ⋘ z_2') \vee$
$(\theta_1 \ll \theta_2 \wedge z_1' ⋘ z_2')$

(3.2-1.4) $z_1 = list(z_1') \wedge z_2 = list(z_2') \wedge z_1' ⋘ z_2'$

(3.2-1.5) $z_1 = record(z_1^1, z_1^2, \ldots, z_1^n) \wedge z_2 = record(z_2^1, z_2^2, \ldots, z_2^m) \wedge$
$m = n \wedge \forall i (1 \le i \le n \rightarrow (z_1^i = z_2^i \vee z_1^i ⋘ z_2^i)) \wedge$
$\exists i (1 \le i \le n \wedge z_1^i ⋘ z_2^i))$.

Note that in (3.2-1.3), the arguments $\theta_1$ and $\theta_2$ are restricted to be within the syntactic category length, and fixed integers or domains as *integer* or *int_intervall* are possible values of these arguments.

Following fig.3.1-2, it holds that *rhombus* « *polygon*, *voronoi_bi* « *property_image*, or *polygon* « $D1, for example. According to definition 3.2-1, from these examples of relation « it follows that

*rhombus* ««« *polygon*,

*voronoi_bi* ««« *property_image*,

*polygon* ««« $D1,

*vector(integer,rhombus)* ««« *vector(integer,polygon)*,

*vector(int_intervall,polygon)* ««« *vector(integer,polygon)*,

*list(polygon)* ««« *list($D1)*, or

*record(list(polygon),voronoi_bi)* «««
*record(list($D1),property_image)*.

The relation ««« is transitive, asymmetric and irreflexive because these properties are true for relation «.

### 3.2.2. Substitutions

A *substitution* $\sigma$ will be defined in the sequel by an ordered set of *replacement rules* $z \to z'$. The application of such a substitution will be defined in such a way that these rules are applied in parallel.

*Definition 3.2-2 (Substitutions* $\sigma_\Theta$ *and* $\sigma_{\mathcal{X}}$*; operand substitution):* A *substitution* $\sigma_\Theta$ *of operand domains* is a finite list of replacement rules $\theta_i \to \theta_i'$,

$$\sigma_\Theta = (\theta_1 \to \theta_1', \ldots, \theta_n \to \theta_n'),$$

with $\theta_i, \theta_i' \in \Theta$ and $\theta_i' \ll \theta_i$, for $i=1,2,\ldots,n$, and $\theta_i \neq \theta_j$ for $i,j=1,2,\ldots,n$ and $i \neq j$. A *substitution* $\sigma_{\mathcal{X}}$ *of operand domain variables* is a finite list of replacement rules $x_i \to x_i'$,

$$\sigma_{\mathcal{X}} = (x_1 \to x_1', \ldots, x_n \to x_n'),$$

with $x_i \in \mathcal{X}_D$ and $x_i' \in \mathbb{DT}$, for $i=1,2,\ldots,n$, and $x_i \neq x_j$ for $i,j=1,2,\ldots,n$ and $i \neq j$. A substitution $\sigma = [\sigma_\Theta \sigma_{\mathcal{X}}]$ is called an *operand substitution*.

Note that always $x_i \ggg x_i'$, for $x_i \in \mathcal{X}_D$ and $x_i' \in \mathbb{DT}$ according to the definition of $\lll$. Substitutions $\sigma_\Theta$ and $\sigma_{\mathcal{X}}$ may be performed independent of each other, and in parallel, i.e. $[\sigma_\Theta \sigma_{\mathcal{X}}]$ is defined.

Applying an operand substitution $\sigma = [\sigma_\Theta \sigma_{\mathcal{X}}]$ on an operand $d(d_t, d_f)$ is defined to be the mapping of $d_t$ onto $\sigma(d_t)$, where for any replacement rule $z \to z'$ of $\sigma$, for each occurence of z in $d_t$ this z is replaced by z' in $\sigma(d_t)$. This syntactic operation is transforming words of the language $\mathbb{DT}$ into words of this language. The application of a substitution is defined in such a way that these rules are applied in parallel.

Let NUM(*pattern*, *string*) be the number of different occurrences as substring of string or symbol *pattern* in word *string*, e.g. NUM(*abba*, *aabbabba*)=2.

*Example 3.2-3:* For example, let $\sigma_\Theta$ = ⟨*polygon*⟶*rhombus*, *rhombus*⟶*rhomb_fill*⟩. Then,

$\sigma_\Theta$(*record*(*polygon*, *list*($X), *rhombus*, $X)) =
*record*(*rhombus*, *list*($X), *rhomb_fill*, $X).

Furthermore, let $\sigma_X$ = ($D→*patient_data*, $X→*rhombus*). Then, sequential application of $\sigma_X$ and $\sigma_\Theta$ leads to

$\sigma_\Theta\sigma_X$(*record*(*polygon*, *list*($X), *rhombus*, $X)) =
$\sigma_\Theta$(*record*(*polygon*, *list*(*rhombus*), *rhombus*, *rhombus*))
*record*(*rhombus*, *list*(*rhomb_fill*), *rhomb_fill*, *rhomb_fill*)

but, for the parallel operand substitution $\sigma=[\sigma_\Theta\sigma_X]$ we have

$\sigma$(*record*(*polygon*, *list*($X), *rhombus*, $X)) =
$[\sigma_\Theta\sigma_X]$(*record*(*polygon*, *list*($X), *rhombus*, $X)) =
$[\sigma_X\sigma_\Theta]$(*record*(*polygon*, *list*($X), *rhombus*, $X)) =
*record*(*rhombus*, *list*(*rhombus*), *rhomb_fill*, *rhombus*).

For example, to demonstrate function NUM it holds that

NUM($X, *record*(*polygon*, *list*($X), *rhombus*, $X)) = 2,

i.e. this function NUM may be used to denotate the number of applications of a replacement rule. ∎

An operand substitution $\sigma=[\sigma_\Theta\sigma_X]$ is defined to be a *non-redundant operand substitutions with respect to operands* $\delta$, $\delta'$, ..., $\delta''$ iff for any replacement rule x→x' in the substitution $\sigma$, the symbol x appears in $d_t$ or $d_t$' or ... or $d_t$'' at least once, i.e. NUM(x, $d_t$)≥1 or NUM(x, $d_t$')≥1 or ... or NUM(x, $d_t$'')≥1.

For example, in substitution $\sigma_X$ of Example 3.2-3, the replacement rule $D→*patient_data* was redundant with respect to $d_t$ = *record*(*polygon*, *list*($X), *rhombus*, $X).

For an operand $\delta$ = $d(d_t, d_f)$ and an operand substitution $\sigma=[\sigma_\Theta\sigma_X]$, let

$$\mathrm{SCP}(\delta,\sigma_\Theta) = \sum_{\theta\to\theta'\in\sigma_\Theta} \mathrm{NUM}(\theta,d_t)*(\chi(\theta)-\chi(\theta')),$$

$$\mathrm{SCP}(\delta,\sigma_X) = \sum_{x\to x'\in\sigma_X} \mathrm{NUM}(x,d_t)*(\chi(x)-\chi(x'))$$

$$= \sum_{x \to x' \in \sigma_{\chi}} \mathrm{NUM}(x, d_t) * (\chi(\theta_{root}) - \chi(x')) \text{ and}$$

$$\mathrm{SCP}(\delta, \sigma) = \mathrm{SCP}(\delta, \sigma_{\Theta}) + \mathrm{SCP}(\delta, \sigma_{\chi})$$

be quantitative evaluations of the *substitution complexity* of these substitutions applied to $\delta$. Because of the factors $\mathrm{NUM}(\theta, d_t)$ or $\mathrm{NUM}(x, d_t)$, redundant replacement rules with respect to $\delta$ are not considered within this evaluation.

*Example 3.2-4:* For example, in the case of fig.3.1-2 and

$d_t$ = *record(polygon, list(rhombus), rhombus, rhombus))*

it holds that

$\mathrm{SCP}(d(d_t, d_f), \{polygon \to rhombus,\ rhombus \to rhomb\_fill\}) =$

$= \chi(polygon) - \chi(rhombus) + 3(\chi(rhombus) - \chi(rhomb\_fill))$

$= \chi(polygon) + 2\chi(rhombus) - 3\chi(rhomb\_fill)$

$= \chi(polygon) + 2\chi(rhombus)$. ∎

### 3.2.3. *Matching and unification of operands*

These basic transformations of operands will be used during program construction for applying rules of the knowledge base of the program space onto the actual state of the program which has to be constructed.

*Definition 3.2-5 (Reduction relation* ▶ *and compatibility relation* ≍ *):* For two program space operands $\delta, \delta' \in \mathbb{L}_D$ with $\delta = d(d_t, d_f)$ and $\delta' = d'(d_t', d_f')$ we define that

(i) $\delta$ *may be reduced to* $\delta'$ (denoted by $\delta ▶ \delta'$), iff $d_f = d_f'$, and there exists an operand substitution $\sigma = \sigma_\Theta \sigma_\chi$ such that

(3.2-2.1) $$\sigma(d_t) = d_t'.$$

(ii) $\delta$ and $\delta'$ are *compatibel* (denoted by $\delta \asymp \delta'$), iff $d_f = d_f'$, and there exists an operand substitution $\sigma = \sigma_\Theta \sigma_\chi$ such that

(3.2-2.2) $$\sigma(d_t) = \sigma(d_t').$$

Note that in Definition 3.2-5 it is not assumed that only non-redundant substitutions with respect to $\delta$ or $\delta'$ are used in equations (3.2-2.1) and (3.2-2.2). The relations ▶ and ≍ are reflexive because the substitutions used in equations (3.2-2.1) and (3.2-2.2) may be empty altogether, i.e. $d_t = d_t'$ would follow.

Thus, if $\delta$ and $\delta'$ are compatibel then both program space operand domains $d_t$ and $d_t'$ may be transformed by consistent replacement rules into the same word $d_t''$ of $\mathbb{DT}$ , and the program space operands $\delta$ and $\delta'$ both may be reduced to $\delta'' = d''(d_t'', d_f'')$ with $d_f'' = d_f = d_f'$, and any descriptor $d'' \in \mathbb{D}$.

*Example 3.2-6:* For example, let

$\delta$ = *array1(vector(integer,vector($D11,$D12)),in)*
$\delta'$ = *array3(vector(10,$D2),in).*

Then there exist substitutions

$\sigma_\chi$ = *<$D2→vector($D11,$D12)>*
$\sigma_\Theta$ = *<integer→10>*

such that equation (3.2-2.2) is satisfied with

$$[\sigma_\Theta \sigma_X](d_t) = [\sigma_\Theta \sigma_X](d_t')$$
$$= vector(10, vector(\$D11, \$D12)).\ \blacksquare$$

The relation ▶ is reflexive, transitive and asymmetric. In the sense of /Golt,Sedg/ the decision whether one program space operand may be reduced to another one, or not, may be seen as a *matching problem*.

> The *matching problem* for program space operands $\delta$, $\delta'$:
>
> For given $\delta$, $\delta'$ with $d_f = d_f'$, are there substitutions $\sigma_\Theta$, $\sigma_X$ such that (3.2-2.1) holds ?

*Theorem 3.2-7:* For two program space operands $\delta, \delta' \in \mathbb{L}_D$ with $\delta = d(d_t, d_f)$ and $\delta' = d'(d_t', d_f')$ it holds that $\delta ▶ \delta'$ iff

$$d_f = d_f' \text{ and } d_t = d_t' \text{ or } d_t \ggg d_t'.$$

*Proof:* It holds that $\delta ▶ \delta'$ iff $d_f = d_f'$ and $d_t = d_t'$ (if $\sigma = ()$ in 3.2-2.1) or $\sigma(d_t) = d_t'$ for $\sigma \neq ()$. The effects of non-empty substitutions $\sigma = \sigma_\Theta \sigma_X$ on words $w \in \mathbb{DT}$ are characterized by the equations (3.2-1.1)...(3.2-1.5). With equation (3.2-1.1) the effect of a replacement rule $\theta \to \theta'$ is described for $\theta, \theta' \in \Theta$ and $\theta' \ll \theta$, and with equation (3.2-2.2) the effect of a replacement rule $x \to x$ is described for $x \in X_D$. The remaining equations (3.2-1.3)...(3.2-1.5) are characterizing the single or repeated application of these both types of replacement rules within *vector*-, *list*-, or *record*-structures. Because there are no further types of structures in the language $\mathbb{DT}$, these equations are complete descriptions of the effects of non-empty substitutions. Thus, $\sigma(d_t) = d_t'$ for $\sigma \neq ()$ is equivalent to $d_t \ggg d_t'$. $\blacksquare$

*Theorem 3.2-8:* For two program space operands $\delta, \delta' \in \mathbb{L}_D$ with $\delta = d(d_t, d_f)$ and $\delta' = d'(d_t', d_f')$ and $\delta ▶ \delta'$ there exists only a finite number of pairwise non-isomorphic words $z \in \mathbb{D}T$ satisfying

$$d_t \ggg z \quad \text{and} \quad z \ggg d_t'.$$

*Proof:* Following Theorem 3.2-7 we assume that $d_t \ggg d_t'$. Based on equations (3.2-1-1)...(3.2-1.5) we may conclude that the number of possible non-isomorphic words $z \in \mathbb{D}T$ satisfying $d_t \ggg z$ and $z \ggg d_t'$ may be characterized by the number of successors (function SUCC) of substrings appearing in $d_t$ and by the number of predecessors (function PRED) of substrings appearing in $d_t'$. This holds because the structure of $d_t$ and $d_t'$, i.e. the structuring by *vector-*, *list-*, or *record*-constructs must be identical in the case $d_t \ggg d_t'$ according to equations (3.2-1.3)-(3.2-1.5). Because of the finite degree of all nodes in the tree $(\Theta,<)$ this number of possible non-isomorphic words $z \in \mathbb{D}T$ is finite. ∎

From Theorem 3.2-7 and Theorem 3.2-8 it follows immediately:

*Corollary 3.2-9:* For two program space operands $\delta, \delta' \in \mathbb{L}_D$ with $\delta \blacktriangleright \delta'$ there exists only a finite number of pairwise non-isomorphic operands $\delta''$ satisfying $\delta \blacktriangleright \delta'' \blacktriangleright \delta'$.

The relation $\equiv$ is reflexive, transitive and symmetric, and thus an equivalence relation. But note that two program space operands may be compatible with respect to different non-redundant operand substitutions $\sigma = \sigma_\Theta \sigma_X'$ or $\sigma' = \sigma_\Theta' \sigma_X'$. Let

$$\text{SUB}(\delta,\delta') = \{\sigma\colon \sigma = [\sigma_\Theta \sigma_X] \wedge \delta = d(d_t, d_f) \wedge \delta' = d'(d_t', d_f) \wedge$$
$$\sigma(d_t) = \sigma(d_t') \wedge \sigma \text{ non-redundant w.r.t. } \delta \text{ and } \delta'\}$$

be the set of all unifying operand substitutions which are non-redundant with respect to $\delta$ and $\delta'$. It follows that

$$\text{SUB}(\delta,\delta') = \emptyset$$

in the case that $\delta$ and $\delta'$ are not compatible.

The decision whether two program space operands are compatible or not, may be seen as a *unification problem*, compare, e.g. , */Golt,Rahm/*. The matching problem represents a "one-sided" unification problem. Two operands are compatible iff they may be reduced to a common operand.

Different operand substitutions in the set SUB($\delta,\delta'$) of all *unifiers* of $\delta$ and $\delta'$ have to be compared for defining a unique *most general unifier* $\sigma \in SUB(\delta, \delta')$ of program space operands $\delta$, $\delta'$

If $\delta'' = d''(\sigma(d_t), d_f)$ is defined according to equation (3.2-2.2), i.e. $\sigma \in SUB(\delta, \delta')$, then $\delta''$ is called a *divisor* of $\delta$ and $\delta'$. During program construction, the descriptors of operands have to be selected in an unique way. Therefore, we shall define that a divisor of $\delta$ and $\delta'$ has always the same descriptor as $\delta$, i.e. $d''=d$. In this way, the notion "divisor of $\delta$ and $\delta'$" is directed and different from "divisor of $\delta'$ and $\delta$".

*Theorem 3.2-10:* For program space operands $\delta, \delta', \delta'' \in \mathbb{L}_D$, if $\delta''$ is a divisor of $\delta$ and $\delta'$, then $\delta \blacktriangleright \delta''$ and $\delta' \blacktriangleright \delta''$.

*Proof:* By definition of a divisor it holds that $\delta''$ is a divisor of $\delta = d(d_t, d_f)$ and $\delta' = d'(d_t', d_f)$ iff there exists an operand substitution $\sigma = [\sigma_\Theta \sigma_X]$ with $\sigma(a_t) = \sigma(d_t')$ where $\sigma$ is non-redundant w.r.t. $\delta$ and $\delta'$. Thus, $\delta \blacktriangleright \delta''$ and $\delta' \blacktriangleright \delta''$ holds w.r.t. the same substitution $\sigma$. ∎

*Definition 3.2-11 (Most general divisor, most general unifier):* Let, $\delta''$ be a divisor of operands $\delta$ and $\delta'$. Then, $\delta''$ is called a *most general divisor* of $\delta$ and $\delta'$ iff there exists no further divisor $\delta^* = d^*(d_t^*, d_f)$, with $d_t''$ non-isomorphic to $d_t^*$, of $\delta$ and $\delta'$ such that $\delta^*$ may be reduced to $\delta''$. For a most general divisor $\delta''$ of $\delta$ and $\delta'$, an operand substitution $\sigma$ non-redundant w.r.t. $\delta$ and $\delta'$ is called a *most general unifier* iff $d_t'' = \sigma(d_t) = \sigma(d_t')$.

According to this definition, formally we may define that

$$MGD(\delta \to \delta') = \{\delta'' : \delta \blacktriangleright \delta'' \wedge \delta' \blacktriangleright \delta'' \wedge \neg\exists \delta^* (\delta^* \in DT \wedge \delta \blacktriangleright \delta^* \blacktriangleright \delta'' \wedge \delta' \blacktriangleright \delta^* \wedge \delta^* \text{ non-isomorphic to } \delta'')\}.$$

Note that the relation "$\delta''$ is a divisor of $\delta$ and $\delta'$" was directed in that sense that the descriptor of $\delta''$ is equal to the descriptor of $\delta$, i.e. all $\delta''$ in the set $MGD(\delta \to \delta')$ do have the same descriptor $d$. In this way, by determining most general divisors a *descriptor substitution*

$$\sigma_D = (d' \to d)$$

is defined. We shall prove that this set MGD($\delta \to \delta'$) contains pairwise isomorphic operands only, i.e. the most general divisor is uniquely determined up to isomorphic renamings of variables. In this sense it is possible to speak about *the* most general divisor.

The most general unifier may be defined to be those substitution which maps onto the most general divisor of the given operands $\delta$ and $\delta'$

A quantitative measure UND($\delta, \delta', \sigma$) expressing the *unification distance* of two compatible operands $\delta$ and $\delta'$ *with respect to substitution* $\sigma = [\sigma_\Theta \sigma_\aleph]$ satisfying equation (3.2-2.2) is introduced by

(3.2-3) $\quad \mathrm{UND}(\delta, \delta', \sigma) = \mathrm{SCP}(\delta, \sigma) + \mathrm{SCP}(\delta', \sigma)$

Then, by

(3.2-4) $$\mathrm{UND}(\delta, \delta') = \begin{cases} \min \{\mathrm{UND}(\delta, \delta', \sigma) : \sigma \in \mathrm{SUB}(\delta, \delta')\} \\ \aleph, \text{ if } \mathrm{SUB}(\delta, \delta') = \emptyset. \end{cases}$$

the *unification distance* of two operands $\delta$ and $\delta'$ is defined. Let $\aleph$ be the symbol of (countable) infinite. Of course, we have UND($\delta, \delta'$) < $\aleph$ iff $\delta$ and $\delta'$ are compatible, i.e. $\delta$ and $\delta'$ have at least one divisor $\delta''$.

> The *unification problem* for program space operands $\delta$, $\delta'$:
>
> For given $\delta$, $\delta'$ with $d_f = d_f'$, are there substitutions $\sigma_\Theta, \sigma_\aleph$ such that equation (3.2-2.2) holds ? If "yes", then the most general divisor of $\delta$ and $\delta'$ has to be computed.

Note that by solving this unification problem, also a descriptor substitution $\sigma_D$ is computed.

For a pair of program space operands $\delta = d(d_t, d_f)$ and $\delta' = d'(d_t', d_f')$ and a divisor $\delta'' = d(d_t'', d_f'')$ of $\delta$ and $\delta'$

with $d_t'' = [\sigma_\Theta \sigma_X](d_t) = [\sigma_\Theta \sigma_X](d_t')$ we say that $\delta''$ is *within unification distance to* $\delta$ *and* $\delta'$ iff $UND(\delta, \delta') = UND(\delta, \delta', \sigma_\Theta \sigma_X)$.

*Theorem 3.2-12 (Unification Theorem):* For any pair of program space operands $\delta$ and $\delta'$, if $\delta$ and $\delta'$ are compatible, then there exists a unique (up to isomorphy) most general divisor $\delta^*$ of $\delta$ and $\delta'$, and it holds that $\delta^*$ is (up to isomorphy) the only operand within unification distance to $\delta$ and $\delta'$.

*Proof:* Let $\delta = d(d_t, d_f)$ and $\delta' = d'(d_t', d_f')$ be two compatible program space operands, i.e. it holds that $d_f = d_f'$, and there exist substitutions $\sigma_\Theta$, $\sigma_X$ such that $[\sigma_\Theta \sigma_X](d_t) = [\sigma_\Theta \sigma_X](d_t') = d_t''$. Thus, for some descriptor $d'' \in \mathbb{D}$, $\delta'' = d(d_t'', d_f)$ is a divisor of $\delta$ and $\delta'$, i.e. the existence of at least one divisor of $\delta$ and $\delta'$ is ensured.

By Corollary 3.2-9, for these program space operands $\delta, \delta'' \in \mathbb{L}_D$ or $\delta', \delta'' \in \mathbb{L}_D$ with $\delta \triangleright \delta''$ or $\delta' \triangleright \delta''$, there exist only finite numbers of pairwise non-isomorphic operands $\delta^*$ satisfying $\delta \triangleright \delta^* \triangleright \delta''$ or $\delta' \triangleright \delta^* \triangleright \delta''$, respectively.

Then, let $\mathbb{M}$ be the set of all program space operands which are the maximum (with respect to relation $\triangleright$) elements contained in both of this finite sets. Thus, for $\delta^* \in \mathbb{M}$ it holds that $\delta \triangleright \delta^* \triangleright \delta''$, $\delta' \triangleright \delta^* \triangleright \delta''$ and there exists no program space operand $\delta'''$, non-isomorphic to $\delta^*$, such that $\delta \triangleright \delta''' \triangleright \delta^*$ and $\delta' \triangleright \delta''' \triangleright \delta^*$. Because of the existence of at least one divisor of $\delta$ and $\delta'$, the set $\mathbb{M}$ is non-empty.

Because of Theorem 3.2-7, for $\delta_1^*, \delta_2^* \in \mathbb{M}$ it holds that $\delta_1^*, \delta_2^*$ are in unification distance $UND(\delta, \delta')$ to $\delta$ and $\delta'$. Let $\delta = d(d_t, d_f)$, $\delta' = d'(d_t', d_f')$ and

$$[\sigma_{i,\Theta} \sigma_{i,X}](d_t) = [\sigma_{i,\Theta} \sigma_{i,X}](d_t') = d_{i,t}^*,$$

for $\delta_i^* = d_i(d_{i,t}^*, d_f)$ and $i=1,2$. If $d_{1,t}^*$ and $d_{2,t}^*$ would be non-isomorphic words, then the substitutions $\sigma_{1,\Theta} \sigma_{1,X}$ and $\sigma_{2,\Theta} \sigma_{2,X}$, could be reduced to substitution $\sigma_\Theta \sigma_X$ such that $\delta^* = d(d_t^*, d_f)$ with

$$[\sigma_{\Theta}\sigma_{X}](d_t) = [\sigma_{\Theta}'\sigma_{X}'](d_t') = d_t^*$$

and $\delta \triangleright \delta^* \triangleright \delta_i^*$ and $\delta' \triangleright \delta^* \triangleright \delta_i^*$. But, this would be a contradiction to the definition of set $\mathbb{M}$. Thus, all $\delta_i^* \in \mathbb{M}$ have to be pairwise isomorphic, i.e. the most general divisor is unique up to isomorphy, and (up to isomorphy) the only operand within unification distance to $\delta$ and $\delta'$. ∎

### 3.2.4. Unification of lists of operands

Program operators which have to be refined during program construction do have several operands as arguments in general. For that reason, we have to consider the case that lists of operands have to be unified for applying a certain refinement rule.

*Definition 3.2-13 (Unification of lists of operands):* A list $l$ of program space operands may be *reduced* to a list $l'$ of program space operands (denoted by $l \blacktriangleright l'$) iff there exists a permutation $\pi$ of the index set $\{1,2,\dots,n\}$ of the list $l'=(\delta_1',\delta_2',\dots,\delta_n')$ such that

$$\delta_i \blacktriangleright \delta_{\pi(i)}'$$

holds, for $l=(\delta_1,\delta_2,\dots,\delta_n)$ and $i=1,2,\dots,n$. Assume that $\delta_i \blacktriangleright \delta_{\pi(i)}'$ according to operand substitution $\sigma_i$. In this case we write

$$l'=\Sigma(l\,|\pi)$$

where $\Sigma=[\sigma_1,\sigma_2,\dots,\sigma_n]$. For $\sigma_i=[\sigma_{\Theta,i}\sigma_{\chi,i}]$ we write $\Sigma_\Theta=[\sigma_{\Theta,1},\sigma_{\Theta,2},\dots,\sigma_{\Theta,n}]$ and $\Sigma_\chi=[\sigma_{\chi,1},\sigma_{\chi,2},\dots,\sigma_{\chi,n}]$ in this case. Two lists $l$ and $l'$ of program space operands are *compatible* (denoted by $l \equiv l'$) iff there exists a permutation $\pi$ of the index set $\{1,2,\dots,n\}$ of the list $l'=(\delta_1',\delta_2',\dots,\delta_n')$ such that

$$\delta_i \equiv \delta_{\pi(i)}'$$

holds, for $l=(\delta_1,\delta_2,\dots,\delta_n)$ and $i=1,2,\dots,n$. Assume that $\delta_i \equiv \delta_{\pi(i)}'$ according to operand substitution $\sigma_i$. In this case we write

$$\Sigma(l)=\Sigma(l'\,|\pi,\sigma_D)$$

where $\Sigma=[\sigma_1,\sigma_2,\dots,\sigma_n]$, and the list $\Sigma(l)$ is a *divisor* of lists $l$ and $l'$. Here,

$$\sigma_D=\sigma_{D,1} \cup \sigma_{D,2} \cup \dots \cup \sigma_{D,n}$$

is the *descriptor substitution* of lists $l$ and $l'$ consisting of descriptor substitutions $\sigma_{D,i}$ of operands $\delta_i$ and $\delta_{\pi(i)}$

The list $\Sigma(l)=l''=(\delta_1'',\ldots,\delta_n'')$ of program space operands is a (up to isomorphy) *most general divisor* of lists $l$ and $l'$ denoted by $MGD(l+l')$ with respect to permutation $\pi$ and descriptor substitution $\sigma_D$ iff $\delta_i''=MGD(\delta_i+\delta_{\pi(i)}')$ is the most general divisor of $\delta_i$ and $\delta_{\pi(i)}'$, for all $i=1,2,\ldots,n$, with $\sigma_{D,i}=(d_{\pi(i)}+d_i)$.

Note that the general divisor may be dependent on the permutation,i.e. different permutations $\pi$ may result into different general divisors of lists $l$ and $l'$, and, of course, certain permutations may not result into any divisor of both lists at all.

Here, the *unification distance* $UND(l,l'|\pi,\Sigma)$ of two lists $l$ and $l'$ of operands, which are compatible with respect to permutation $\pi$ and operator substitution $\Sigma$, is defined by

$$UND(l,l'|\pi,\Sigma) = \frac{1}{n}\sum_{i=1}^{n} UND(\delta_i,\delta_{\pi(i)}',\sigma_i)$$

for lists of length n and $\Sigma=[\sigma_1,\sigma_2,\ldots,\sigma_n]$. If $\sigma_i^*$ is a most general unifier of $\delta_i,\delta_{\pi(i)}'$, for $i=1,2,\ldots,n$, then $\Sigma^* = [\sigma_1^*,\sigma_2^*,\ldots,\sigma_n^*]$ is a most general unifier for lists $l$ and $l'$ according to permutation $\pi$. Let

$$UND(l,l'|\pi) = UND(l,l'|\pi,\Sigma^*)$$

be in this case.

### 3.3 Unification of Operators

The definitions and conclusions related to matching and unification of operators are closely related to those given and drawn in the previous section for operands.

A program space operator was defined to be a word $f(f_t, l)$ of the language $\mathbb{L}_F$, with $f \in \mathbb{F}$, $f_t$ and $l$ are in the syntactic categories operator_domain and **operands** respectively. For example,

*scan(tv_scan,[pict($D1,out),w_par($D2,in_out)])* or

*user_request($F1,[request(string,in),ans(boolean,out)])*

are words of the language $\mathbb{L}_F$, i.e. program space operators with

$f_t$ = *tv_scan*
and $l$ = *[pict($D1,out),w_par($D2,in_out)]*, or

$f_t$ = $F1
and $l$ = *[request(string,in),ans(boolean,out)]*,

respectively.

Because the descriptor $f \in \mathbb{F}$ is nothing else than a unique name of the given operator $f(f_t, l)$, in the following we shall say that operators $f(f_t, l)$ and $f'(f_t, l)$ are *isomorphic*. Furthermore, if $f_t$ and $f_t'$, or $l$ and $l'$ are different just by different names of variables, also the operators $f(f_t, l)$ and $f'(f_t', l')$ are *isomorphic*.

*Definition 3.3-1 (Substitutions $\sigma_{\Phi}$ and $\sigma_{\mathbb{X}}$, operator substitution): A substitution $\sigma_{\Phi}$ of operator domains* is a finite list of at most two replacement rules $\phi_i \to \phi_i'$,

$$\sigma_{\Phi} = (\phi_1 \to \phi_1', \ldots, \phi_n \to \phi_n'),$$

with $\phi_i, \phi_i' \in \Phi$ and $\phi_i' \ll \phi_i$, for $i=1,2,\ldots,n$, and $\phi_i \neq \phi_j$ for $i,j=1,2,\ldots,n$ and $i \neq j$. A *substitution $\sigma_{\mathbb{X}}$ of operator domain variables* is a finite list of at most two replacement rules $x_i \to x_i'$,

$$\sigma_{\mathbb{X}} = (x_1 \to x_1 \ , \ldots, x_n \to x_n'),$$

with $x_i \in \mathcal{X}_F$ and $x_i' \in (\mathcal{X}_F \cup \Phi)$, for $i=1,2,\dots,n$, and $x_i \neq x_j$ for $i,j=1,2,\dots,n$ and $i \neq j$. An *operator substitution* is given by $\sigma=[\sigma_\Phi \sigma_\mathcal{X}]$.

Note that always $x_i \gg x_i'$, for $x_i \in \mathcal{X}_F$ and $x_i' \in \Phi$ according to the definition of $\ll$, but $x_i \gg x_i'$ is not true for $x_i \in \mathcal{X}_F$ and $x_i' \in \mathcal{X}_F$ because the specification relation is not reflexiv, i.e. $\phi_{root} \ll \phi_{root}$ is not true. Substitutions $\sigma_\Phi$ and $\sigma_\mathcal{X}$ may be performed independent of each other, and in parallel, i.e. $\sigma=[\sigma_\Phi \sigma_\mathcal{X}]$ is defined.

Applying an operator substitution $\sigma=[\sigma_\Phi \sigma_\mathcal{X}]$ to an operator $f(f_t, l)$ is defined to be the mapping of $f_t$ onto $\sigma(f_t)$, where for any replacement rule $z \to z'$ of $\sigma$, for an occurence of z in $f_t$ this z is replaced by z' in $\sigma(f_t)$. This syntactic operation is transforming words of the syntactic category operator_domain into words of this syntactic category.

Note that transformations of the operand-parts were considered in Section 3.2.

In the sequel we shall assume that only *non-redundant operator substitutions* $\sigma=[\sigma_\Phi \sigma_\mathcal{X}]$ *with respect to operators* $f(f_t, l)$ *and* $f'(f_t', l')$ are used if a substitution is considered for these operators, i.e. for any replacement rule $x \longrightarrow x'$ in the substitutions $\sigma_\Phi, \sigma_\mathcal{X}$ the symbol x appears in $f_t$ or in $f_t'$, i.e. $\sigma$ contains two replacement rules at most.

For an operator $\varphi = f(f_t, l)$ and an operator substitution $\sigma=[\sigma_\Phi \sigma_\mathcal{X}]$, let

$$SCP(\varphi,\sigma_\Phi) = \sum_{\phi \to \phi' \in \sigma_\Phi} NUM(\phi, f_t)*(\chi(\phi)-\chi(\phi')),$$

$$SCP(\varphi,\sigma_\mathcal{X}) = \sum_{x \to x' \in \sigma_\mathcal{X}} NUM(x, f_t)*(\chi(x)-\chi(x'))$$

$$= \sum_{x \to x' \in \sigma_\mathcal{X}} NUM(x, f_t)*(\chi(\phi_{root})-\chi(x')), \text{ and}$$

$$SCP(\varphi,\sigma) = SCP(\varphi,\sigma_\Phi) + SCP(\varphi,\sigma_\mathcal{X})$$

be quantitative evaluations of the *substitution complexity* of these substitutions $\sigma_{\Phi}$, $\sigma_{\mathfrak{X}}$ and $\sigma$ applied to $\varphi$.

*Definition 3.3-2 (Reduction relation* $\blacktriangleright$ *and compatibility relation* $\equiv$ *):* For two program space operators $\varphi, \varphi' \in \mathbb{L}_F$ with $\varphi = f(f_t, l)$ and $\varphi' = f'(f_t', l')$ we define that

(i) $\varphi$ *may be reduced to* $\varphi'$ (denoted by $\varphi \blacktriangleright \varphi'$), iff $l \blacktriangleright l'$, and there exists an operator substitution $\sigma = [\sigma_{\Phi} \sigma_{\mathfrak{X}}]$ such that

(3.3-1.1) $$\sigma(f_t) = f_t'.$$

(ii) $\varphi$ and $\varphi'$ are *compatibel* (denoted by $\varphi \equiv \varphi'$), iff $l \equiv l'$, and there exists an operator substitution $\sigma = [\sigma_{\Phi} \sigma_{\mathfrak{X}}]$ such that

(3.3-1.2) $$\sigma(f_t) = \sigma(f_t').$$

Note that in Definition 3.3-2 it is assumed that only non-redundant substitutions with respect to $\varphi$ or $\varphi'$ are used in equations (3.3-1.1) and (3.3-1.2). The relations $\blacktriangleright$ and $\equiv$ are reflexive because the substitutions used in equations (3.3-1.1) and (3.3-1.2) may be empty altogether, i.e. $f_t = f_t'$ would follow.

If equation (3.3-1.1) holds then $\sigma = \langle f_t \rightarrow f_t' \rangle$. If $\varphi$ and $\varphi'$ are compatibel then both program space operator types $f_t$ and $f_t'$ may be transformed by consistent substitutions into the same word $f_t''$ of the syntactic category operator_domain which is called a *divisor* of $f_t$ and $f_t'$, the lists $l$ and $l'$ may be transformed into a general divisor $l''$ by consistent substitutions including a descriptor substitution $\sigma_D$, and the program space operators $\varphi$ and $\varphi'$ both may be reduced to an operator $\varphi'' = f(f_t'', l'')$ also applying a *descriptor substitution*

$$\sigma_F = \langle f' \rightarrow f \rangle$$

for the mapping of the operator descriptor of $\varphi'$ onto that of operator $\varphi$. Note that this reduction is directed in the sense of descriptor substitutions.

Similarily to Definition 3.2-11, a divisor $f_t''$ of $f_t$ and $f_t'$ is called a *most general divisor* of $f_t$ and $f_t'$ denoted by MGD($f_t \rightarrow f_t'$) iff there exists no further divisor $f_t^*$ of $f_t$

and $f_t$' with $f_t$' non-isomorphic to $f_t^*$ such that $f_t^*$ may be reduced to $f_t$'.

*Example 3.3-3:* For example, let

$\varphi$ = *scan($F1,[window_coo(int_array,in_out),pict($D1,out)])*

and

$\varphi$' = *scan_tv($F2,[picture($D2,out)]),w_par($D3,in_out)])* .

Then there exist an operator substitution

$$\sigma = [\langle \$F1 \rightarrow scanning, \$F2 \rightarrow scanning \rangle]$$

and an operand substitution

$$\Sigma = [[\langle \$D1 \rightarrow \$D2 \rangle],[\langle \$D3 \rightarrow int\_array \rangle]]$$

with a permutation $\pi$, $\pi(1)=2$ and $\pi(2)=1$ such that equation (3.3-1.2) is satisfied and the operand lists are compatible according to $\Sigma$ and $\pi$ . ∎

By the extension of relation ≡ given in definition 3.3-2, the relation ≡ remains reflexive, transitive and symmetric.

The decision whether two program space operators are compatible or not represents the *unification problem* that has to be solved during operator refinement.

If $\varphi'' = f(\sigma(f_t),\Sigma(l'|\pi,\sigma_D))$ is defined according to equation (3.3-1.2) and $\Sigma(l)=\Sigma(l'|\pi,\sigma_D)$ is a divisor of lists $l$ and $l'$, then $\varphi''$ is called a *divisor* of $\varphi$ and $\varphi'$. $\sigma_D$ and $\sigma_F$ are the corresponding descriptor substitutions.

*Definition 3.3-4 (Most general divisor, most general unifier):* Let, $\varphi'' = f(f_t'',l'')$ be a divisor of operators $\varphi$ and $\varphi'$ Then, $\varphi''$ is called a *most general divisor* of $\varphi$ and $\varphi'$ denoted by $MGD(\varphi \rightarrow \varphi')$ iff $f_t''=MGD(f_t \rightarrow f_t')$ is a most general divisor of $f_t$ and $f_t'$ and $l''=MGD(l \rightarrow l')$ is a most general divisor of operand lists $l$ and $l'$of operators $\varphi$ and $\varphi'$. For a most general divisor $\varphi'' = f(\sigma(f_t),\Sigma(l))$ of $\varphi$ and $\varphi'$, the substitution quadruple

$$MGU(\varphi \rightarrow \varphi')=[\sigma,\Sigma,\sigma_D,\sigma_F]$$

is called a *most general unifier* for operators $\varphi$ and $\varphi'$.

The most general unifier $MGU(\varphi \rightarrow \varphi')$ is uniquely determined up to isomorphy.

A quantitative measure $UND(\varphi,\varphi' | \sigma,\pi,\Sigma)$ expressing the *unification distance* of two compatible operators $\varphi$ and $\varphi'$ with respect to operator substitution $\sigma=[\sigma_{\Phi}\sigma_{\mathfrak{X}}]$, permutation $\pi$ and operand substitution $\Sigma$ is defined by

(3.3-2) $$UND(\varphi,\varphi' | \sigma,\pi,\Sigma) = SCP(\varphi,\sigma) + SCP(\varphi',\sigma) + UND(l,l' | \pi,\Sigma)$$

where $l$ and $l'$ are the operand lists of $\delta$ and $\delta'$. We have $UND(\varphi,\varphi' | \sigma,\pi,\Sigma) < \aleph$ iff $\varphi$ and $\varphi'$ are compatible.

> The *unification problem* for program space operators $\varphi,\varphi'$:
>
> For given $\varphi$, $\varphi'$ are there an operator substitution $\sigma$, a permutation $\pi$ and an operand substitution $\Sigma$ such that both operators may be unified applying $\sigma$, $\pi$ and $\Sigma$ ? If "yes" then the most general divisors of operator types $f_l$ and $f_l'$ and of lists $l$ and $l'$ have to be computed.

This unification problem has to be solved during program construction repeatedly. Performing a unification includes the transformation of descriptors of the second operator into descriptors of the first operator formally given by substitutions $\sigma_D$ and $\sigma_F$.

### 3.4. Constraints

Program schemes are partial descriptions of *subgoals* or operators one construction level before which were refined into these corresponding program schemes. The description of program schemes may be supplemented by *global constraints* which limit the set of allowable bindings of variables $f \in \mathcal{X}_F$ and $d \in \mathcal{X}_D$, i.e., these constraints are characterizing the decision space of all available alternatives within the program space. There are two types of constraints which are relevant to our approach of program construction - *informational constraints* which may be expressed by relations between operand domains of the program space, and in the most simple situation these constraints are expressions formulated with the help of the predicate calculus with operand domains as arguments and relations like SAME, SPECIALISATION_OF etc. or *functional constraints* which express relations between operator domains of the program space in a similar manner.

Let $\mathbb{REL}$ be a set of relations RELAT defined on the interpreted sets $\Xi(\Theta)$ and $\Xi(\Phi)$ which are either general ones, e.g. the specification relation denotatet by SPECIALISATION_OF$\in\mathbb{REL}$ or the identity relation SAME$\in\mathbb{REL}$, or specific in areas of application defined on certain tuples of domains only. This relations RELAT$\in\mathbb{REL}$ are considerd to have a fixed semantics with respect to $\Xi(\Theta)$ and $\Xi(\Phi)$.

Let $\mathbb{R}_C$ be a set of relation symbols which are used as terminal ones within our syntactic approach. Symbols $relat \in \mathbb{R}_C$ are interpreted by relations

$$\Xi(relat) = \text{RELAT} \in \mathbb{REL}.$$

To simplify our denotations, we assume this correspondence between *italics* and CAPITALS to be a fixed representation of such an interpretation $\Xi$, e.g. the symbol $same \in \mathbb{R}_C$ is interpreted by the identity relation SAME$\in\mathbb{REL}$.

*Example 3.4-1:* For example, the informational constraint

*same*($Segment_type,$Component_type)

ensures the identity of the operand domains of the operand

*segment*($Segment_type,*in_out*)

and of the components of the operand

*segment_class_list*(*vector*($Dimension,$Component_type),*in*).

The functional constraint

*specialisation_of*($Operator_domain,*merge*)

points out that the operator domain of the operator

*calculate_sum_of_areas*($Operator_domain,
[*areas*($D,in),sum(integer,out)])

must be a specialization of a general *merge* operator domain. ∎

The binding of unbound operator and/or operand domain variables of program schemes is restricted by *constraints* during program construction. Constraints are words of a language $\mathbb{L}_C(\mathbb{G}_C)$ with the productions shown in fig. 3.4-1.

The terminal alphabet of the constraint language $\mathbb{L}_C(\mathbb{G}_C)$ is given by

$$\mathbb{T}_C = \{,,(,),not,and,or\} \cup \mathbb{X}_F \cup \mathbb{S} \cup \mathbb{X}_D \cup \Theta \cup \mathbb{R}.$$

*Definition 3.4-1 (Satisfyability of constraints):* A constraint $\gamma\in\mathbb{L}_C(\mathbb{G}_C)$ is called *satisfied* iff $\gamma$ does not contain any variable and is true with respect to the fixed interpreted relations of $\mathbb{R}$ (according to interpretation $\mathbb{D}$). A constraint $\gamma\in\mathbb{L}_C(\mathbb{G}_C)$ is called *satisfyable* iff there exists a variable binding which replaces all operand domain variables and all operator domain variables appearing in $\gamma$ by operand domain symbols and operator domain symbols, respectively, such that the resulting constraint is true with respect to the fixed interpreted relations of $\mathbb{R}$.

Note that any satisfied constraint is also satisfyable (with respect to the empty variable binding).

The way of application of constraints during the

$P_{33}$: constraint $\longrightarrow$ relation ( arguments )
$\mathbb{R}(P_{33}) = \langle constraint.\chi \leftarrow arguments.\chi \rangle$

$P_{34}$: $constraint_1 \longrightarrow$ *not* ( $constraint_2$ )
$\mathbb{R}(P_{34}) = \langle constraint_1.\chi \leftarrow constraint_2.\chi \rangle$

$P_{35}$: $constraint_1 \longrightarrow$ *and* ( $constraint_2$ , $constraint_3$ )
$\mathbb{R}(P_{35}) = \langle constraint_1.\chi \leftarrow constraint_2.\chi + constraint_3.\chi \rangle$

$P_{36}$: $constraint_1 \longrightarrow$ *or* ( $constraint_2$ , $constraint_3$ )
$\mathbb{R}(P_{36}) = \langle constraint_1.\chi \leftarrow constraint_2.\chi + constraint_3.\chi \rangle$

$P_{37}$: arguments $\longrightarrow \langle f \in \mathcal{X}_F \rangle , \langle f' \in \mathcal{X}_F \rangle \mid$
$\langle f \in \mathcal{X}_F \rangle , \langle f' \in \mathfrak{F} \rangle \mid$
$\langle f \in \mathfrak{F} \rangle , \langle f' \in \mathcal{X}_F \rangle$
$\mathbb{R}(P_{37}) = \langle arguments.\chi \leftarrow \chi(f) + \chi(f') \rangle$

$P_{38}$: arguments $\longrightarrow \langle d \in \mathcal{X}_D \rangle , \langle d' \in \mathcal{X}_D \rangle \mid$
$\langle d \in \mathcal{X}_D \rangle , \langle d' \in \Theta \rangle \mid$
$\langle d \in \Theta \rangle , \langle d' \in \mathcal{X}_D \rangle$
$\mathbb{R}(P_{38}) = \langle arguments.\chi \leftarrow \chi(d) + \chi(d') \rangle$

$P_{39}$: relation $\longrightarrow \langle REL \in \mathbb{R} \rangle$
$\mathbb{R}(P_{39}) = \langle \rangle$

*Fig. 3.4-1: Productions of grammar* $\mathbb{G}_C(\mathbb{N}_C, \mathbb{T}_C, \mathbb{P}_C, constraint)$.

refinement process will be explained later on. Here, this grammar is completing our syntactic definitions of basic objects of our approach to program construction.

Constraints may be seen under different points of view. Besides an operand or operator selection function, constraints are used for representing relations between objects, or interactions between subgoals and as a part of the description of the program schemes generated so far. Constraints are used by design operators during specifying their construction activities and are operands of the program space. The generation and satisfaction of constraints are performed by *constraint processing operators* of the design space and will be a subject of Section 4.

The prototypical operands or operators of the program space knowledge base are compared by design operators with operands or operators of the actual program to be constructed considering relevant constraints and the result of such comparisions are *differences* (e.g the unification distance UND) which summerize the distance of a given program object to a prototypical knowledge unit as well as to a complete instance of this object. Besides other quantitative measures like complexity $\chi$ these differences represent objects of the design space and are used by strategy space operators to support the next design activities.

### 3.5 *Knowledge Base and Program Construction*

The knowledge base of the program space contains *signature-structure rules* which are describing admissible refinements of program space operators, and *data-structure rules* which are specifying admissible refinements of program space operand data types.

The signature-structure rules are represented by triples

(trans, cons, sem)

where trans denotes the transformation, i.e. a production

**operator → program_scheme**

which will be called a *signature-structure production*. Here, operator is a syntactic category of language $\mathbb{L}_F$ and program_scheme is a syntactic category of the language $\mathbb{L}_S$, i.e. the *premise* of this transformation is a word of the language $\mathbb{L}_F$ and the *conclusion* is a word of the language $\mathbb{L}_S$. The constraint cons is a word of the language $\mathbb{L}_C$, i.e. within the syntactic category constraint. An informal description of the signature's semantics is represented by sem without restricting the syntax of sem at this point.

The data-structure rules are represented by tuples

(trans, cons)

where the transformation trans is a production

**operand_domain → compound_type**

and will be called a *data-structure production*. Data-structure rules are mapping words of the syntactic category operand_domain into the syntactic category compound_type of language $\mathbb{L}_D$ considering the constraint cons$\in\mathbb{L}_C(\mathbb{G}_C)$ where the grammar $\mathbb{G}_C$ was defined in fig. 3.4-1. But, constraints in data-structure rules are restricted in such a sense that rules $P_{37}$ are not applied for generating such a constraint cons, i.e. the terminal alphabet for these rules does not contain elements of the sets $\mathcal{X}_F$ or $\Phi$.

Data-structure rules allow to expand the data type structure alternatively to their specification.

Some remarks to the sem-part of signature-structure rules: Generally speaking, sem may be evaluated for enabeling *user controlled selection*, i.e. a signature-structure production may be additionally labeled by any informal descriptions characterizing their application domain oriented usage and effect, particularly to determine the semantics connected to the order of the left hand side operands.

These descriptions sem may contain also operand and/or operator descriptors which have to be replaced by a string equivalent to actual operator_type and/or data_type bindings by the system-user interface. The examples of fig. 3.5-1 and fig. 3.5-2 illustrate these definitions. Note the correspondence of the operand *pict* in the signature and structure parts of the given signature-structure rule. It is

(i)

**trans** *results* → *list(record($D, features, statistics))*

**cons** *or(same($D, patient_name), same($D, identification_key))*

(ii)

**trans** *image* → *vector(256, vector(256, greyvalue))*

**cons** *true*

(iii)

**trans** $D → *vector(2, integer)*

**cons** *specialization($D, coordinates)*

*Fig. 3.5-1: Examples of data-structure rules.*

**trans**

```
cardio(img_proc,[pict(image,inout)])
➡
begin
 set(set_const,[ans(boolean,out),val(true,in)]);
 while ans(boolean,in) do
  begin
   scan(tv_scan,[pict($I,out)]);
   process(image_proc,[pict($I,in),
                              res(histogram,out)]);
   user_request($X,[request(string,in),
                           ans(boolean,out)])
  end
end.
```

**cons** *specialization($X,yes_no_request)*

**sem** *'processing of %pict% by %cardio%'*

*Fig. 3.5-2: Example of signature-structure rule.*

a neccessary condition for these rules that each operand of operator has to appear with the same descriptor and with the same data-type value in **program_scheme** also, the data-flow type may be different. The cons-part of fig. 3.5-2 constraines the operator domain of *user_request* to be a specialization of the operator domain *yes_no_request*.

The variables within the sem-parts of the

signature-structure rules denoted by $\%x\%$ with $x \in \mathbb{F}$ or $x \in \mathbb{D}$ express that there will be a substitution of these constructs by the domain of x during rule instantiation.

The general representation within the program space is the introduced program scheme language $\mathbb{L}_S$. The actual stage of the program to construct consists of the corresponding program scheme *P* and a set of *global unresolved constraints* $\mathbb{C}$ which is to be considered to be a conjunction of satisfyable constraint expressions according to fig. 3.4-1 and which were set up by design space operators during the program construction process. At the beginning of a program construction process, the set $\mathbb{C}$ is empty. During program construction, all constraints of the applied signature-structure or data-structure rules are used to update the set $\mathbb{C}$.

The construction of programs is performed by subsequent scheduling of refinement and specification steps.

In case of *specification* the actual program scheme *P* is examined for nonterminal operator and/or operand domains which have to be transformed by further evaluations. Nonterminal operator domains $\phi \in \Phi$ with $SUCC(\phi) \neq \emptyset$ or $f \in \mathcal{X}_F$ then will be replaced by some $\phi' \in SUCC(\phi)$ or $\phi' \in SUCC(\phi_{root})$, respectively. Nonterminal operand domains $\theta \in \Theta$ with $SUCC(\theta) \neq \emptyset$ or $d \in \mathcal{X}_D$ will be replaced by some $\theta' \in SUCC(\theta)$ or $\theta' \in SUCC(\theta_{root})$, respectively.

*Refinement* of operands or operators of the actual program scheme *P* can be performed by applying signature-structure or data-structure rules of the knowledge base.

Let

$$\mathcal{X}(w) = \{\, x \mid (x \in \mathcal{X}_D \vee x \in \mathcal{X}_F) \wedge NUM(x,w) \geq 1 \,\}$$

be the common set of domain variables occuring within the word w and

$$\mathcal{Y}(w) = \{\, y \mid (y \in \Gamma \vee y \in \mathbb{F}) \wedge NUM(y,w) \geq 1 \,\}$$

be the common set of operand and operator descriptors occuring within the word w. For avoiding undesirable variable correspondences a renaming function RENAME(w, w') is introduced for mapping syntactic expressions w into isomorphic expressions RENAME(w,w') with $\mathfrak{X}$(RENAME(w,w'))∩$\mathfrak{X}$(w')=∅ and $\mathfrak{Y}$(RENAME(w,w'))∩$\mathfrak{Y}$(w')=∅. Here we do not specify how this function may be selected, it suffices at this point that such a unique mapping exists. A function REPLACE(w,s,s') produces a word w' with substring s' in place of substring s of word w.

Considering the refinement of an operand

$$\delta=d(d_t,d_f)$$

of program scheme $P$ by a data-structure rule

$$\rho=(t,c) \text{ with } t=(d_t{}'\to d_t{}'')\text{,}$$

at first we transform $\rho$ into the renamed rule

$$\rho^*=\text{RENAME}(\rho,P)=(t^*,c^*) \text{ with } t^*=(d_t{}^{*\prime}\to d_t{}^{*\prime\prime})\text{.}$$

The refinement of $\delta$ by applying $\rho$ is syntactically possible according to equation 3.2-2.2 and Definition 3.4-1 if there exists a most general unifier $\sigma=[\sigma_\Theta\sigma_\mathfrak{X}]$ such that

$$\sigma(d_t)=\sigma(d_t{}^{*\prime})$$

and, considering the set $\mathbb{C}$ of global constraints build up so far,

$$\sigma_\mathfrak{X}(\mathbb{C}\cup(c^*)) \text{ is satisfyable.}$$

Applying rule $\rho$ the actual program scheme $P$ is transformed into $P'$ denotated by

$$P \;-\rho\text{->}\; P'$$

and the actual set of global constraints $\mathbb{C}$ is transformed into $\mathbb{C}'$ denoted by

$$\mathbb{C} \;-\rho\text{->}\; \mathbb{C}'$$

with

$$P'=\sigma_\mathfrak{X}(\text{REPLACE}(P,d_t,\sigma(d_t))) \text{ and}$$

$$\mathbb{C}'=\sigma_\mathfrak{X}(\mathbb{C}\cup c^*)\text{,}$$

where $\mathbb{C}'$ may be simplified in general if, e.g. $c^*$ represents a "sub-constraint" of a constraint existing in $\mathbb{C}$ already.

Considering the refinement of an operator

$$\varphi=f(f_{t},l)$$

of program scheme $P$ by a signature-structure rule

$$\rho=(t,c,s) \qquad \text{with} \qquad t=(\varphi'\to P'),$$

at first we transform $\rho$ into the the renamed rule

$$\rho^{*}=\text{RENAME}(\rho,P)=(t^{*},c^{*},s^{*}) \qquad \text{with} \qquad t^{*}=(\varphi^{*}{}'\to P^{*}{}').$$

The refinement of $\varphi$ by applying $\rho$ is syntactically possible according to Definitions 3.3-4 and 3.4-1 if there exists a most general unifier $\text{MGU}(\varphi\to\varphi^{*}{}')=[\sigma,\Sigma,\sigma_{D},\sigma_{F}]$ and $\sigma_{\mathbb{X}}\Sigma_{\mathbb{X}}(\mathbb{C}\cup(c^{*}))$ is satisfyable, considering the actual set $\mathbb{C}$ of global constraints.

The sem-part of $\rho$ will be instantiated by applying substitutions $\sigma_{D}$ and $\sigma_{F}$ and by replacing %x% in the sem-part by the domain symbol of x.

Applying rule $\rho$ the actual program scheme $P$ is transformed into $P''$ denotated by

$$P \;-\rho\!\to\; P''$$

and the actual set of global constraints $\mathbb{C}$ is transformed into $\mathbb{C}'$ denoted by

$$\mathbb{C} \;-\rho\!\to\; \mathbb{C}'$$

with

$$P''=\sigma_{\mathbb{X}}\Sigma_{\mathbb{X}}(\text{REPLACE}(P,f_{t},\sigma\Sigma\sigma_{D}\sigma_{F}(P^{*}{}')))$$

and

$$\mathbb{C}'=\sigma_{\mathbb{X}}\Sigma_{\mathbb{X}}(\mathbb{C}\cup(c^{*})).$$

For examples of program scheme specification and refinement see Appendix 2.

## 4. The Inference Machine

The inference machine has the general task to map the actual state of the constructed program onto a succeeding state where the general goal consists in derivating a design state such that any operator or operand is completely refined. Based on this final design state, the modul P_GEN will map the generated program representation into the target language.

The activities within the problem space are characterized by interactive processing of semantic complexes of conditions, and the activities within the program space are characterized by construction steps to refine and specify the actual hierarchy of program schemes. Both activities and the cooperation between them are controlled by the inference machine based, e.g., on the the correspondence relations represented in the connection table. By following this way, the program space may be considered to be independent of the problem space.

## *4.1 The Design Space*

The design of computer programs may be considered to be an iterative and hierarchical construction process where the principle of subseauent decompositions of complex processing tasks into funtionally relatively closed but cooperating subtasks represents the methodological basis, see fig.4.1-1. This design approach is performed by repeated application of the operators where each operator may be split into three phases,

MATCH to find out the set of applicable design operators,

SELECT to schedule a subset of the design operators found, and

ACTivate to apply design operators following some general advice.

In each decomposition or refinement step a complex task will be mapped onto a structure of functional and/or data nodes by selecting prototype operators and/or operands of the program space and instantiating the corresponding program subscheme (structure). Specification of the program schemes set up so far may be performed by constraint satisfaction. Without functional constraints between operators of the program space, the functional nodes of such a structure would be functionally independent and are labeled by operators which are working on adjacent data nodes representing their arguments. Following this approach, relations between functional nodes would be restricted to organizational ones specified by the given structure of the program scheme and to informational ones as specified by connections via data nodes or via informational constraints. Under the given assumption only informational relations have to be considered during the refinement of a functionally independent operator. This approach will be used as a "first attempt" to solve the refinment problem.

As an alternative to the decomposition of complex

operators by refinement *specification operators* of the design space are reducing directly the difference of nonterminal program objects to terminal ones. A *complete instance* of any program object is given if it can be mapped by the program generator P_GEN into the target programming language. Levels of specification are used for a quantitative evaluation of the distance of a given instance to a complete instance. The original concept has maximum distance to a complete instance in comparison to all the

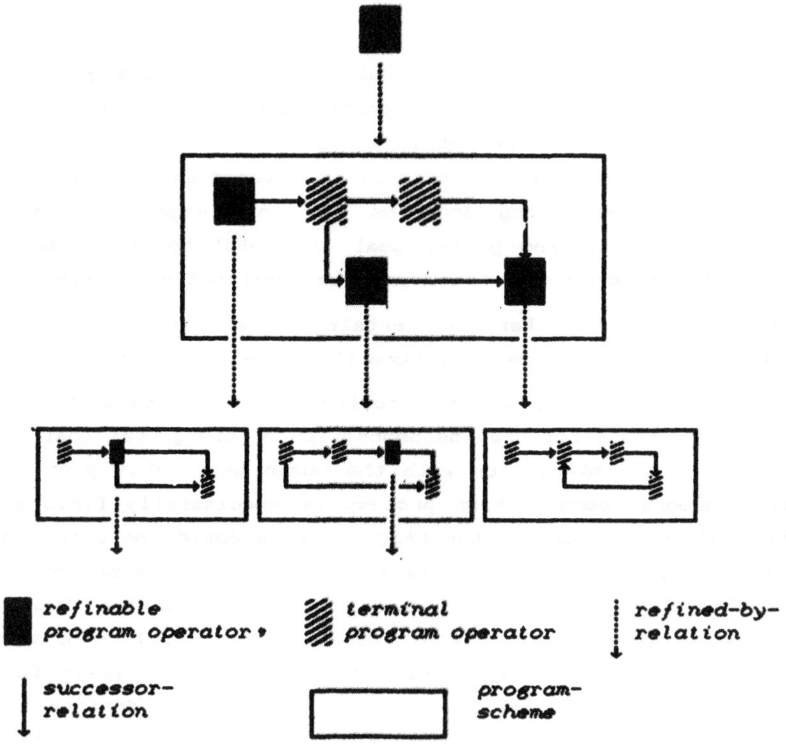


*Fig. 4.1-1: Program refinement hierarchy.*

*partial instances* appearing between concept and complete instance during the design process.

By *refinement operators*, operator instances of the program space will be decomposed into suboperands and suboperators. It is the key idea of *hierarchical construction* that operators representing subgoals will be refined into specific schemes containing more specific operands and operators at subsequent *levels of construction*. Top-level zero represents the start situation, level 1 of the program construction process is describing the rough *program scheme* in coincidence with the specified global goal where all functional nodes of such a program scheme are labeled by operator instances of the program space which may be viewed as subgoals, and all data nodes of such a program scheme are labeled by operand instances of the program space, deeper levels of the construction process represent program schemes in more and more detail.

To illustrate this approach it is assumed that within the context of generating programs for any image processing system the following global goal 'is told' to the problem space of the knowledge based program construction system:

**"Scan a picture. Perform certain operations within the image. Ask wether a next picture should be analyzed."**

At the beginning of the problem specification a 'rough draft' of the structural decomposition of the global goal is generated by interaction with the human user. This part of the program construction process is successfully finished if a prototype rule of the program space could be selected and a program scheme could be set up which may be placed at construction level 1 by refinement operators of the design space. In this initial stage, specification operators of the design space may be activated from the strategy space for specifying nonterminal operator and/or operand domains by automatic constraint processing or user request. This initial stage may result in the following program scheme shown in fig. 4.1-2.

```
begin
set(set_const,[ans(boolean,out),val(true,in)]);
while ans(boolean,in) do
  begin
  scan(tv_scan,[pict(image,out)]);
  process(image_proc,[pict(image,in),res($D,out)]);
  user_request($F,[request(string,in),ans(boolean,out)])
  end
end.
```

*Fig. 4.1-2: Example of program scheme at construction level 1.*

In this structure four operators of the program space, *set*, *scan*, *process* and *user_request*, and five operands of the program space specified by their symbolic names *val*, *pict*, *res*, *request* and *ans* are structurally and informationally connected. The operator *set* and the operands *ans* and *val* are fully specified, i.e., they are labeled by terminal operator or operand domains and may be transformed by the program generator P_GEN into the source code of the target programming language immediately. The operators *scan*, *process*, *pict*, *res* and *request* are partially specified, whereas the domain of the operator *user_request* is completely unspecified. After that further specification on level 1 or refinement of nonterminal operators or operands may be performed according to the strategy of program construction. Constraints are used to specify relations between operators or between operands which are represented by certain instances within the program schemes generated up to a given moment. Because these constraints are formulated without restrictions by the organisational connections of these program schemes, in general they are used to specify such relations between operators and between operands which may be not ensured within these program schemes.

Following the conventional *top-down-approach* of designing

complex systems by designing subsystems which then may be specified nearly independently as the main direction of stepwise refinement of subgoals, also some construction mechanisms are directed *bottom-up*. For example the special operator *CHECK* of the design space for constraint processing may be activated from strategy space and the result may be that an over-constrained situation is reported. In this case, the special operator *BACKTRACK* is used to delete over-constrained instances of objects or operators as well as its refinement schemes. Here, a sophisticated solution for making goal-directed decisions (*partial* deletion of instances of objects or operators, or specifications within these units) is a research issue of further work. So far, circular reasoning with repeated appearances of the same overconstrained situation is hard to avoid in general. Here, the *least commitment strategy /Ste1,Ste2/* seems to be the best heuristic principle for specifying design operators for avoiding backtracking situations by defering decisions when they are under-constrained. Less dramatic than backtracking, bottom-up mechanisms are contained in specification operators for specifying operator or operand instances in dependence of construction levels below.

Program schemes may be mapped by generator P_GEN into a completely specified program in the target programming language. In such a final state, all the operators of the program scheme are either

(i) *target* ones which may be mapped by the program generator P_GEN into the target programming language, or

(ii) recognized to be labeled with the same operator domain as one of its predecessors in the refinement hierarchy (case of *recursive procedures*), or

(iii) labeled with the same operator domain as an operator (case (i)) which is not a predecessor in the refinement hierarchy (not case (ii)), and the operator complexity $\chi$ is 'sufficient large' (case of a

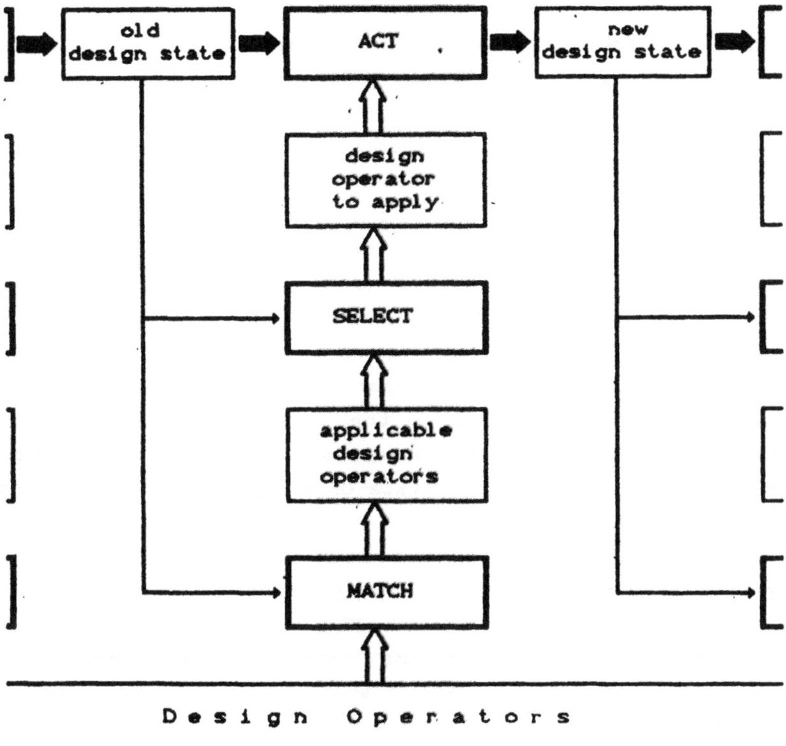


*Fig. 4.1-3: General design step with basic* MATCH-SELECT-ACT *cycle.*

*universal subroutine*).

Note that the target operators may be at different levels of the program scheme reflecting different levels of construction. For case (iii) we consider the measure $\chi$ and its different possibilities of specification, i.e. the selection of the maximum complexity, or the averaged complexity etc. as well as the selection of the $k$-constants $k_{op}$, $k_{while}$ etc. which were introduced in Section 3.1.2.

The process of program construction may be considered as performing subsequent *design steps* as presented in fig.4.1-3. Generally each design step is organized as a basic MATCH-SELECT-ACT *cycle*. The *current state of the design process* is represented by the updated *data base*, the actual *program* constructed so far, the existing *global constraints*, and the *design history*.

During the MATCH phase the design state will be compared with design operators checking their preconditions of applicability. As the result of this matching process a reduced set of *applicable design operators* will be set up.

Dependent on strategy space operators, during the SELECT-phase a target space operator will be choosen which is the *operator to apply* to the current design state for transforming it into a *new design state* which in most cases is much closer to the goal state of the program construction process.

During the ACT-phase the operator selected will be applied effecting the actual design state. Besides the aim of conflict resolution each SELECT action is connected to a *push operation* to store the rest of the alternatives produced by MATCH as design history for later resuming in case of *backtracking*.

This MATCH-SELECT-ACT cycle occurs at different levels with certain modifications because of the *hierarchically organized decision process* during one design step.

Figures 4.1-4 to 4.1-6 are showing parts of the decision tree of a single design step. Even one of the applicable suboperators created by the MATCH-phase can be activated by the ACT-phase according to the strategic decision, made by the SELECT-phase. In the following a brief description of the effects of the design operators of figures 4.1-4 to 4.1-6 is given.

### *4.1.1. Design step*

There are two basic high level operators in fig.4.1-4 which can be activated at the beginning of a certain design step, *GO_FORWARD* or *GO_BACKWARD*.

Such a design step consists of three different design phases which are characterized as follows:

(α) **MATCH-phase**

(1) *GO_FORWARD* is applicable if

(1.1) at least there exists one operator which is evaluated by a nonterminal or nontarget operator domain or

(1.2) at least there exists one operand which is evaluated by a nonterminal or nontarget operand domain or

(1.3) there exists any unresolved global constraint.

(2) *GO_BACKWARD* is applicable if

(2.1) the design history is not empty.

(β) **SELECT-phase**

The Selection may be triggered by the human user or by the result of an investigation of the global constraints for an underconstrained or an overconstrained - no valid substitution of domains can be found - situation.

(γ) **ACT-phase**

(1) *GO_FORWARD* is forcing the program construction process and is causing any refinement or specification step to reduce the difference between the current state and the goal state of the program to construct.

(2) *GO_BACKWARD* initiates backtracking setting back the program state to a former one and resuming stored alternatives of former design decisions from the design history.

These design steps are performed till a certain *termination criterion* is satisfied. The program construction process is finished if

(i) all operators are evaluated by target operator domains, and

(ii) all operands are evaluated by target operand domains or by data structures (*list*, *vector*, *record*) which contain only target operand domains, and

(iii) all operands which appear only with data flow relation *in* are evaluated by operand domains which are both target and terminal ones, and

(iv) no unresolved global constraints exist.

In the following, basic design operators will be described by characterizing their MATCH-, SELECT-, and ACT-phases.

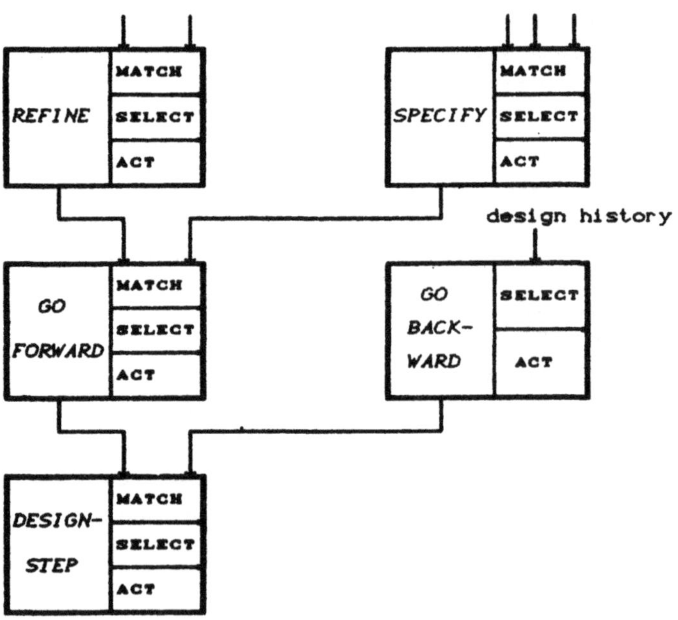


*Fig. 4.1-4: Design operator hierarchy (decision tree - part 1).*

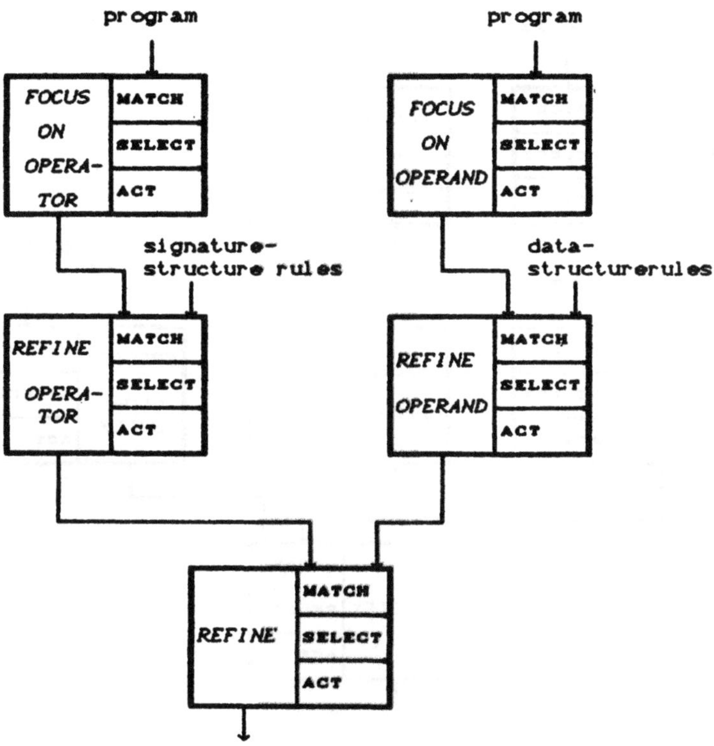


*Fig. 4.1-5: Design operator hierarchy (decision tree - part 2).*

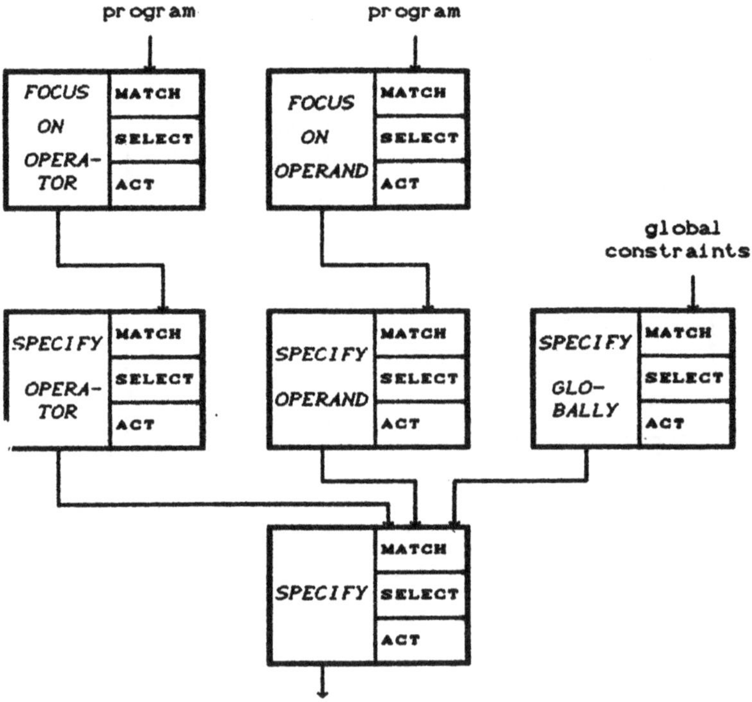


*Fig. 4.1-6: Design operator hierarchy (decision tree - part 3).*

### *4.1.2. Design step operators*

*There* are three basic design operators or top-level design operators, *GO_FORWARD*, *GO_BACKWARD* and *FOCUS_ON_OPERATOR/OPERAND*.

(1) *GO_BACKWARD*-operator

(1.α) This operator has no MATCH-phase.

(1.β) Specification of SELECT-phase

SELECT chooses the backtrack goal point within the design history. This point may be located on different decision levels of one former design step.

(1.γ) Specification of ACT-phase

This high level design operator is tracking back to a former SELECT situation and reproduces the respective design state by using the design history. After that this SELECTion will be reactivated with the stored alternatives of the design history.

(2) *GO_FORWARD*-operator

(2.α) Specification of MATCH-phase

MATCH is proving the applicability of the high level suboperators *REFINE* and *SPECIFY*.

*REFINE* is applicable if

(i) at least there exists one operator which is evaluated by a nontarget operator domain or

(ii) at least there exists one operand which is evaluated by a nontarget operand domain.

*SPECIFY* is applicable if

(i) at least there exists one operator which is evaluated by a nonterminal operator domain or

(ii) at least there exists one operand which is evaluated by a nonterminal operand domain or

(iii) there exists any unresolved global constraint.

(2.$\beta$) Specification of SELECT-phase:

As trigger criteria of this selection are used:

(i) the complexity $\chi(P)$ of the actual program $P$ and
(ii) complexity $\chi(\gamma)$ of global constraints $\gamma$.

(2.$\gamma$) Specificatio of ACT-phase:

According to the design strategy either a refinement step for continuing the decomposition process of the program will be performed, or further specifications of operators or operands of the actual program will be done.

The *SPECIFY*- and *REFINE*-operators of the design space are not top-level operators are characterized as follows:

(2.1) *SPECIFY*-operator

(2.1.$\alpha$) Specification of MATCH-phase

MATCH is proving the applicability of the suboperators *SPECIFY_OPERATOR*, *SPECIFY_OPERAND* and *SPECIFY_GLOBALLY*.

*SPECIFY_OPERATOR* is applicable if

at least there exists one operator which is evaluated by a nonterminal operator domain.

*SPECIFY_OPERAND* is applicable if

at least there exists one operand which is evaluated by a nonterminal operand domain.

*SPECIFY_GLOBALLY* is applicable if

there exists any unresolved global constraint.

(2.1.$\beta$) Specification of SELECT-phase

As trigger criteria of this selection are used:

(i) the number and complexity $\chi(f)$ of focusable operators,
(ii) the number and complexity $\chi(d)$ of focusable operands,
(iii) the complexity $\chi(\gamma)$ of global constraints $\gamma$.

(2.1.$\gamma$) Specification of ACT-phase:

According to the design strategy specifications of operator

domains or operand domains of the actual program will be performed.

(2.1.1) *SPECIFY_OPERATOR*-operator

(2.1.1.α) Specification of MATCH-phase

Here it is to find possible specifications of an operator domain symbol $\phi \in \Phi$ or $x \in \mathcal{X}_F$. This will be done by retrieving the approbriate subtree of $(\Phi, <)$ which has the symbol $\phi$ or the most general domain symbol $\phi_{root}$ as the root respectively.

(2.1.1.β) Specification of SELECT-phase

The selection of the subdomain $\phi'$ which must be a specialization of $\phi$ with $\phi' \ll \phi$ or of x with $\phi' \in \Phi$ is performed by displaying the above mentioned subtree to the user and requesting her or his decision.

(2.1.1.γ) Specification of ACT-phase

The original subdomain $\phi$ will be replaced by the new one $\phi'$ or x will be bound to $\phi'$.

(2.1.2) *SPECIFY_OPERAND*-operator

(2.1.2.α) Specification of MATCH-phase

Here it is to find possible specifications of an operand domain symbol $\theta \in \Theta$ or $x \in \mathcal{X}_D$. This will be done by retrieving the respectable subtree of $(\Theta, <)$ which has the symbol $\theta$ or the most general domain symbol $\theta_{root}$ as the root respectively.

(2.1.2.β) Specification of SELECT-phase

The selection of the subdomain $\theta'$ which must be a specialization of $\theta$ with $\theta' \ll \theta$ or of x with $\theta' \in \Theta$ is performed by displaying the above mentioned subtree to the user and requesting her or his decision. In case of parameters which occurs exclusively in the data flow relation in parameter request structures of the problem space are used for requesting the parameter's value from the user or any other source of information.

(2.1.2.$\gamma$) Specification of ACT-phase

The original subdomain $\theta$ will be replaced by the new one $\theta'$ or x will be bound to $\theta'$

(2.1.3) *SPECIFY_GLOBALLY*-operator

(2.1.3.$\alpha$) Specification of MATCH-phase

Here the existing global constraints are investigated to find specifying variable bindings which satisfy the global constraints to reduce the number and/or the complexity $\chi$ of the actual given global constraints by resolving them at least partially.

(2.1.3.$\beta$) Specification of SELECT-phase

If there have been found several lists of variable bindings a selection may be performed by investigating their effects to complexity reduction or by user interaction similar to the design operators *SPECIFY_OPERATOR* and *SPECIFY_OPERAND*.

(2.1.3.$\gamma$) Specification of ACT-phase

The selected variable bindings will be applied resolving the global constraints.

(2.2) *REFINE*-operator

(2.2.$\alpha$) Specification of MATCH-phase

MATCH is proving the applicability of the suboperators *REFINE_OPERATOR* and *REFINE_OPERAND*.

*REFINE_OPERATOR* is applicable if

> at least there exists one operator which is evaluated by a non-target operator domain.

*REFINE_OPERAND* is applicable if

> at least there exists one operand which is evaluated by a non-target operand domain.

(2.2.$\beta$) Specification of SELECT-phase

As trigger criteria of this selection are used

(i) the number and complexity $\chi(f)$ of focusable operators,
(ii) the number and complexity $\chi(d)$ of focusable operands.

(2.2.$\gamma$) Specification of ACT-phase

According to the design strategy either an attempt to continue the decomposition process of the program by operator or operand refinement will be made.

(2.2.1) *REFINE_OPERATOR*-operator

(2.2.1.$\alpha$) Specification of MATCH-phase

This activity consists in matching the focused operator against the signatures of the signature-structure rules of the program space knowledge base in order to find the most general divisor according to Section 3.2 of this paper which must not violate the local constraint linked with the rule and the existing global constraints. All matching signature-structure rules become members of the set of applicable refinement rules.

The refinement of an operator $\varphi$ appearing in a signature-structure rule

**(operator → program_scheme,cons,sem)**

is possible iff

(i) there exists a most general divisor $\delta^*$ of $\delta$ and operator, i.e. operator$\equiv\delta$ holds, and
(ii) the constraint cons is satisfied.

(2.2.1.$\beta$) Specification of SELECT-phase

The selection activity tries to eliminate the very rule to apply. This will be done in two steps:

(i) Verification of the problem space preconditions connected to each rule over the connection table of the inference machine by activating the data base manager of the problem space machine, and

(ii) strategic selection of the rule to apply if step (i) has lead to more than one applicable rules considering different trigger criteria like the unification distance UND introduced in Sections 3.2 and 3.3.

The connection table of the inference machine is simply a table with two columns where each row contains a pair of pointers to the corresponding parts of problem and program space.

(2.2.1.$\gamma$) Specification of ACT-phase

During the ACT phase the instantiated and selected rule will be applied to refine the focused operator of the program. The actual program will be updated by replacing the operator domain by the instantiated right hand side of the applied rule and by extending the scope of unresolvable parts of the local constraint to be global.

The refinement of an operator may be performed by replacing the operator domain by **program_scheme** and setting up the constraint cons as global valid.

(2.2.2) *REFINE_OPERAND*-operator

(2.2.2.$\alpha$) Specification of MATCH-phase

This activity consists in matching the focused operand domain against the left hand parts of the data-structure rules of the program space knowledge base in order to find the most general divisor according to Section 3.2 of this paper which must not violate the local constraint linked with the rule and the existing global constraints. All matching data-structure rules become members of the set of applicable refinement rules.

An operand $\delta = d(d_t, d_f) \in \mathbb{L}_D(\mathbb{G}_D)$ with $d_t \in \mathbb{DT}$ is refineable by applying a data-structure rule

**(operand_domain → compound_type,cons,sem)**

iff

(i) there exists a most general unifier $\delta^*$ of $\delta$ and **operand_domain**, i.e. **operand_domain**$\equiv\delta$ holds, and

(ii) the constraint cons is satisfied.

(2.2.2.β) Specification of SELECT-phase

The selection activity tries to eliminate the very rule to apply. This will be done in two steps:

(i) Verification of the problem space preconditions connected to each rule over the connection table of the inference machine by activating the data base manager of the problem space machine, and

(ii) strategic selection of the rule to apply if step (i) leads to more than one applicable rules considering different trigger criteria like the unification distance UND introduced in Section 3.2.

(2.2.2.γ) Specification of ACT-phase

During the ACT phase the selected rule will be applied to refine the focused operand of the program. The actual program will be updated by replacing the domain of the focused operand by the right hand side of the instantiated rule and by extending the scope of unresolvable parts of the local constraint to be global.

The refinement of an operand may be performed by replacing the operand domain by **compound_type** and setting up the constraint cons as globally valid.

(3) *FOCUS_ON_OPERATOR/OPERAND*-operator

(3.α) Specification of MATCH-phase

Searching for operators/operands of the actual program which allow the application of the next design operator according to fig. 4.1-4 and 4.1-5.

(3.β) Specification of SELECT-phase

Selecting one of the operators/operands found according to different possible trigger criteria like operator's/operand's complexity $\chi$ or user interaction, and according to basic strategies like depth-first or breadth-first program construction.

(3.γ) Specification of ACT-phase

Supplying the selected operator/operand to the succeeding design operator.

### 4.2 *The strategy space*

All the design space operators are scheduled by the strategy space controlling the SELECT activities of the design operators dependent on quantitative measures as $\chi$ and UND of the design space. In dependence on the actual design situation appropriate design space operators may be activated according to the implemented strategy. First ideas lead to a *least commitment strategy* according to */Ste1,Ste2/*.

Generally spoken it is a very complicated task to find strategy algorithms which are appropriate to control the program construction process in a way that it is comprehensive enough to the human user. Up to now we do not have any model describing usefull programming strategies of human programmers nor we have models for the description the influence of several formal strategic control mechanisms to the general behavior of knowledge based program construction. The strategic desicion space for scheduling design space operators of the proposed concept is very large because of the number of introduced design operators and the diversity of quantitative evaluations characterizing the design state of the program and the possibilities of going forward in the program construction process like unification distance UND, constraint complexity $\chi$, program scheme complexity $\chi$, or the number of unresolved constraints.

So far experimental investigations seem to be the most appropriate way to come closer to a satisfyable solution of the program construction strategy problem. We are orienting on a critical evaluation of different strategies within our next project report.

In Appendix 2, some suggestions about strategy space specifications are contained.

## 5. *Implementation*

The implementation of the discussed knowledge based program construction system is influenced by several points of view, some contradicting one another as testing different approaches, realizing AI methods and demonstrating the efficient, user-friendly, real-time etc. interaction with the run-time system, for example.

During the elaboration of the approach described in this paper several versions of implementation were created each of them corresponding to the actual state of the concept at a certain time. The recent operational version */Hes1/* of the system was implemented in *Pascal* by taking care about the time complexity of subprocesses within the system, some essential progress could be realized in obtaining acceptable computing time behavior. However, the flexibility of the system had to be reduced to ensure a high construction speed. Operators of strategy and design space are hard-wired procedures of the system's kernel. This operational system has a knowledge base in the program space, e.g., for analyzing cardiologic images (target language FORTRAN), an other knowledge base for constructing programs for synthesis design in organic chemistry (target language C and based on the programs within the expert system approach RDS */Bied/*), and an other knowledge base for simplifying data bank treatment (target language dBase).

This operational system variant typically designs programs of about 5 pages of source code within 10 to 20 minutes. During this process of program construction program schemes are displayed in graphical representation in one window and further windows on display are defined by the user interface temporarily. The user has the special opportunity to generate partially (!) specified programs by calling the program generator P_GEN and these programs run by replacing under-constrained domains of the program schemes by default or dummy symbols. The generated programs are easily to understood because of their well-structured shape and the extensive use of comments.

First experiences in practical prototypical applications could be collected in generating image processing programs in medicine */Hes2/*.

Favoring the aspect of using the system for testing mechanisms of program construction as described in this paper, further implementation activities are directed to a more sophisticated implemented version of the system take care that the complete concept proposed in this paper will be met. The prototyping of the next version was started on the basis of Common LISP.

As powerful as a general approach of knowledge based systems is, also in our project it became already clear that the input and modification of knowledge is a key issue. Here, our general approach is to hide as much as possible the implemented structures in order to avoid too technically oriented dialogues. For example, to input a new program scheme just by serial specification of components is the best way to obtain a 'chaotic knowledge base Here, our efforts are directed to flexible representation of contextual knowledge which is selected during the process of knowledge acquisition for demonstrating relations to existing contents as well as for copying existing structures if possible. Much attention was paid to ensure the *consistency* of the knowledge base supervising the insertion and modification of knowledge pieces to dedect multiple-used rules or endless deduction cycles.

The extended version to be completely implemented in the near future will be both a practically applicable tool for comfortable managing and flexible configuration of domain specific software and a powerful research vehicle for studying the nature of computer-aided program construction in general and especially for the investigation of the influence of different strategy mechanisms to the systems behavior.

## 6. Conclusions

In this paper a specific approach to the construction of programs is described. So far it could be proved that programs may be generated by interactive dialogues with high flexibility and reasonable speed. The quality of these programs depends upon the actual contents of the knowledge base, and has to be evaluated independently of the performance of the expert system shell realizing the strategy and design operators. Today we consider the problem of hierarchical and iterative program construction to be solvable by the described construction mechanism and by the described model of program schemes. But for increasing its flexibility the modularity of the implemented version has to be improved. The implementation of a new extended version was started in Common LISP recently.

Flexibility in the program space is characterized by the processes performed during a single refinement step, i.e. how specification and refinement activities may be used to map a prototypical operator onto a complete instance of a program subscheme. Our research is focusing on increasing flexibility in design and strategy space for obtaining this desired flexibility in the program space.

## *References*

*/Bied/* Biedka,K.,J.Streubel,A.Weise, Reaction Design by Synthon Substitution .Arbeitsbericht, Zentralinstitut fuer Kybernetik und Informationsprozesse, Berlin, 1988.

*/Fran/* Franova,M., An implementation of program synthesis from formal specifications: PRECOMAS. Proc. ECAI'88, European Conference on Artificial Intelligence, Munich, August 1-5, 1988, 565 -570.

*/Goet/* Goettler,H., Graphgrammatiken in der Softwaretechnik. Informatik Fachberichte Nr. 178, Springer, 1988.

*/Golt/* Goltz,H.-J.,H.Herre, Mathematische Grundlagen der logischen Programmierung. Informatik-Reporte, Akademie der Wissenschaften der DDR, Institut fuer Informatik und Rechentechnik, Heft 5 1987.

*/Hes1/* Hesse,R.,R.Klette, Automatisierte Programm konstruktion (1). ZKI-Information 3/1987, Akademie der Wissenschaften der DDR, Berlin.

*/Hes2/* Hesse,R.,R.Klein,R.Klette, Knowledge based program construction for image analysis. in: Proceedings, CAIP'87, Wismar, DDR, September 1987, Mathematical Research, Band 40, Akademie-Verlag Berlin 1987, 133 - 140.

*/Hopc/* Hopcroft,J.E.,J.D.Ullman, Introduction to Automata Theory, Languages, and Computation. Addison-Wesley Publishing Company, Reading, Massachusetts, 1979.

*/Krag/* Kragl,G., Eine Programmierumgebung fuer verteiltes Pearl. Arbeitsberichte des Instituts fuer Mathematische Maschinen und Datenverarbeitung, Universitaet Erlangen, Band 19, Nummer 8, Oktober 1986.

*/Man1/* Manna,Z.,R.Waldinger, Knowledge and reasoning in program synthesis. in: Programming Methodology, Springer-Verlag, Berlin Heidelberg New York London Paris Tokyo (LNCS 23), 1975, 236 - 277.

*/Man2/* Manna,Z.,R.J.Waldinger, Synthesis: dreams => programs. SRI International, Techn.Note 156, November 1977.

*/Man3/* Manna,Z.;Waldinger,R.: A deductuve Approach to Program Synthesis. ACM Trans. Progr. Lang. Syst. 2(1980), 90 - 121.

*/Rahm/* Rahmstorf,G.(Hrsg.), Wissensrepraesentation in Expertensystemen. Proceedings, Workshop, Herrenberg, Maerz 1987, Informatik-Fachberichte 172, Springer-Verlag, Berlin Heidelberg New York London Paris Tokyo, 1987.

*/Rech/* Rechenberg,P., Ein neues Maß für die softwaretechnische Komplexität von Programmen. Informatik Forsch. Entw. 1 (1986), 26-37.

*/Sace/* Sacerdoti,E.D., A Structure for Plans and Behavior. Artificial Intelligence Series, Elsevier/Noth-Holland, Amsterdam 1977.

*/Sedg/* Sedgewick,R., Algorithms. Addison-Wesley Publishing Company, Reading, Massachusetts, 1983.

*/Ste1/* Stefik,M., Planning with Constraints (MOLGEN: Part 1). Artificial Intelligence 16(1981), 111-140.

*/Ste2/* Stefik,M., Planning and Metaplanning (MOLGEN: Part 2). Artificial Intelligence 16(1981), 141-169.

*/Wilk/* Wilkins,D.E., Hierarchical planning: Definition and Implementation. in: Proc. of ECAI'86, Milano, Italy, 1986, 466-478

## *List of Symbols*

(i) Mathematical notation

### Grammars and languages

| | |
|---|---|
| $\mathbb{G}=(\mathbb{N},\mathbb{T},\mathbb{P},S)$ | grammar with set $\mathbb{N}$ of variables A,B,C,..., set $\mathbb{T}$ of terminals *a,b,c*,..., set $\mathbb{P}$ of productions $p_1,p_2,p_3,\ldots$ and start symbol $S\in\mathbb{N}$ |
| $\mathbb{V}=\mathbb{N}\cup\mathbb{T}$ | vocabulary of grammar $\mathbb{G}$ |
| $\mathbb{V}^{*}=\mathbb{V}^{+}\cup(\varepsilon)$ | set of words $w_1,w_2,\ldots$ |
| $\varepsilon$ | empty word |
| $\mathbb{L}(\mathbb{G})$ | language generated by grammar $\mathbb{G}$ |
| $AG=(\mathbb{G},\mathbb{A},\mathbb{R},\mathbb{C})$ | attributed grammar with context free grammar $\mathbb{G}$, the set $\mathbb{A}$ of attributes, the set $\mathbb{R}$ of attributation rules, and the set $\mathbb{C}$ of conditions |
| $\mathbb{A}(x)$ | set of attributes defined on symbol $x\in\mathbb{V}$ |
| x.ATT | attribute ATT of symbol x |
| $\chi$ | complexity attribute |

### Sets, relations, functions

| | |
|---|---|
| $\mathbb{N}_0$ | set of natural numbers |
| $\mathbb{R}^{+}$ | set of the positive reals |
| card($\mathbb{A}$) | cardinality of set $\mathbb{A}$ |
| $\aleph$ | cardinality of countable infinite |
| $\langle cond(a)\rangle$ | definition of alternatives of elements *a* satisfying the unary relation *cond* |
| $\mathbb{L}(x)$ | set of leaf nodes of subtree with root x |
| PRED(x) | unique predecessor of x within a tree |
| SUCC(x) | set of successors of x within a tree |
| NUM(u,v) | number of appearances of substring u in string v |
| $\pi$ | permutation |
| FG | FG(a)=F(G(a)), sequential application of |

| | |
|---|---|
| | function G and F |
| [FG] | parallel and independent application of functions F and G, if defined |
| $\sigma$ | substitution |
| $z \rightarrow z'$ | replacement rule of a substitution |

(ii) Problem space

| | |
|---|---|
| CDS | communication data structure |
| $\mathbb{K}$ | set of keys of application area |
| $\mathbb{R}_{key}$ | set of binary relations which are defined onto the set $\mathbb{V}_{key} \times \mathbb{V}_{key}$ of a certain key **key** |
| $\mathbb{V}_{key}$ | set of allowable problem space values with respect to a certain key **key** |
| $\mathbb{R}_C$ | relation symbols for constraints |
| *same*, *specialization* | elements of $\mathbb{R}_C$ |
| $\Xi$ | semantic interpretation |
| $\mathbb{REL}$ | relations on $\Xi(\Theta)$ and $\Xi(\Phi)$ |
| $\mathbb{G}_P(\mathbb{N}_P, \mathbb{T}_P, \mathbb{P}_P, condition)$ | grammar of conditions |
| $\mathbb{L}_P(\mathbb{G}_P)$ | language of conditions $\chi_1, \chi_2, \ldots$ |

(iii) Program space

| | |
|---|---|
| $\delta = d(d_\iota, d_f)$ | operand $\in \mathbb{L}_D$ with $d \in \mathbb{D}$, $d_\iota$ and $d_f$ are in the categories data_type and data_flow |
| $\iota = (\delta_1, \ldots, \delta_n)$ | list of operands |
| $\varphi = f(f_\iota, \iota)$ | operator $\in \mathbb{L}_F$ with $f \in \mathbb{F}$, $f_\iota$ and $\iota$ are in the categories operator_domain and operands |
| $\mathbb{D}$ | set of operand descriptors D, \$D, ... |
| $\mathbb{F}$ | set of operator descriptors F, \$F, ... |
| $\mathbb{X}$ | set of domain variables with $\mathbb{X} = \mathbb{X}_F \cup \mathbb{X}_D$ |
| $\mathbb{X}_F$ | set of operator domain variables $f_1, f_2, \ldots$ |
| $\mathbb{X}_D$ | set of operand domain variables $d_1, d_2, \ldots$ |
| $\Phi$ | set of operator domain symbols $\phi_1, \phi_2, \ldots$ |
| $\Theta$ | set of operand domain symbols $\theta_1, \theta_2, \ldots$ |
| *boolean* | element of $\Theta$ |

| | |
|---|---|
| « | specialization relation for domain symbols and variables |
| $\phi_{root}$, $\theta_{root}$ | most general domains |
| $\mathbb{G}_D(\mathbb{N}_D, \mathbb{T}_D, \mathbb{P}_D, operand)$ | grammar of operands |
| $\mathbb{G}_F(\mathbb{N}_F, \mathbb{T}_F, \mathbb{P}_F, operator)$ | grammar of operators |
| $\mathbb{G}_S(\mathbb{N}_S, \mathbb{T}_S, \mathbb{P}_S, program\_scheme)$ | grammar of program schemes |
| $P$ | program scheme |
| $\mathbb{G}_C(\mathbb{N}_C, \mathbb{T}_C, \mathbb{P}_C, constraint)$ | grammar of constraints |
| $\gamma$ | constraint |
| $\mathbb{L}_D(\mathbb{G}_D)$ | language of operands |
| $\mathbb{DT}$ | language generated by the grammar $\mathbb{G}_D(\mathbb{N}_D, \mathbb{T}_D, \mathbb{P}_D, data\_type)$ |
| $\mathbb{L}_F(\mathbb{G}_F)$ | language of operators |
| $\mathbb{L}_S(\mathbb{G}_S)$ | language of program schemes |
| $\mathbb{L}_C(\mathbb{G}_C)$ | language of constraints |
| P_GEN | program generator, maps into target language |
| DISP | distance of specialization |

(iv) Matching and unification

| | |
|---|---|
| »» | specification relation on $\mathbb{DT}$ |
| ▶ | reduction relation |
| ≡ | compatibility relation |
| $\sigma_\Theta$ | substitution of operand domain symbols |
| $\sigma_\Phi$ | substitution of operator domain symbols |
| $\sigma_\mathbb{X}$ | substitution of domain variables |
| $\Sigma=[\sigma_1, \ldots, \sigma_n]$ | list of substitutions |
| SCP | substitution complexity |
| $SUB(\delta_1, \delta_2)$ | set of unifying substitutions |
| UND | unification distance |
| MGD | most general divisor |
| $MGU(\varphi \to \varphi') = [\sigma, \Sigma, \sigma_D, \sigma_F]$ | most general unifier |

(v) Program construction steps

| | |
|---|---|
| RENAME | renaming function |
| $\rho$=(trans, cons, sem) | signature-structure rule, trans is |

| | |
|---|---|
| | a production operator→program_scheme |
| %x% | variable in sem |
| $\rho$=(trans,cons) | data-structure rule, trans is a production operand_domain→compound_type |
| $\mathbb{C}$ | set of global constraints during a program construction process |
| $P - \rho \rightarrow P'$ | program construction step |
| $\mathbb{C} - \rho \rightarrow \mathbb{C}'$ | updating of set $\mathbb{C}$ |

## *Appendix 1: Derivation Example*

In this appendix, an example of a derivation of words using the grammar $\mathbb{G}_S(\mathbb{N}_S,\mathbb{T}_S,\mathbb{P}_S,\text{program\_scheme})$ is given.

1. Start of the derivation process:

   [program_scheme]

2. Application of production P19:

   *begin* [statements] *end* .

3. Application of production P21:

   *begin* statement ; [statements] *end* .

4. Application of production P21:

   *begin* statement ; statement ; [statements] *end* .

5. Application of production P20:

   *begin* statement ; statement ; [statement] *end* .

6. Application of production P24:

   *begin* statement ; statement ; [structure] *end* .

7. Application of production P27:

   *begin* statement ; statement ; [repetition] *end* .

8. Application of production P30:

   *begin*
   statement ; statement ;
   *while* b_operand *do* [statement]
   *end* .

9. Application of production P24:

   *begin*
   statement ; statement
   *while* b_operand *do* [structure] *end* .

10. Application of production P25:

```
begin
 statement ; statement ;
 while b_operand do
  begin [statements] end
end .
```

11. Application of production P21:

```
begin
 statement ; statement ;
 while b_operand do
  begin statement ; [statements] end
end .
```

12. Application of production P21:

```
begin
 statement ; statement ;
 while b_operand do
  begin statement ; statement ; [statements] end
end .
```

13. Application of production P21:

```
begin
 statement ; statement ;
 while b_operand do
  begin
   statement ; statement ; statement ; [statements]
  end
end .
```

14. Application of production P20:

```
begin statement ; statement ;
 while b_operand do
  begin
   statement ; statement ; statement ; [statement]
  end   end .
```

15. Application of production P24:

```
begin statement ; statement ;
 while b_operand do
  begin
   statement ; statement ; statement ; [structure]
  end
end .
```

16. Application of production P28:

```
begin statement ; statement ;
 while b_operand do
  begin
   statement ; statement ; statement ;
   if b_operand [selection] ;
  end
end .
```

17. Application of production P29:

```
begin statement ; statement ;
 while b_operand do
  begin
   statement ; statement ; statement ;
   if b_operand then statement else [statement]
  end
end .
```

18. Application of production P24:

```
begin statement ; statement ;
 while b_operand do
  begin
   statement ; statement ; statement ,
   if b_operand then statement else [structure]
  end
end .
```

19. Application of production P25:

```
begin statement ; statement ;
 while b_operand do
  begin
   statement ; statement ; statement ;
   if b_operand then statement
   else begin [statements] end
  end
end .
```

20. Application of production P21:

```
begin statement ; statement ;
 while b_operand do
  begin
   statement ; statement ; statement ;
   if b_operand then statement
   else begin statement ; [statements] end
  end
end .
```

21. Application of production P20:

```
begin statement ; statement ;
 while b_operand do
  begin
   statement ; statement ; statement ;
   if b_operand then statement
   else begin statement ; [statement] end
  end
end .
```

22. Application of production P24:

```
begin statement ; statement ;
 while b_operand do
  begin
   statement ; statement ; statement ;
   if b_operand then statement
   else begin statement ; [structure] end
  end
end
```

23. Application of production P26:

```
begin statement ; statement ;
 while b_operand do
  begin
   statement ; statement ; statement ;
   if b_operand then statement
   else
    begin
     statement ;
     if b_operand [selection]
    end
  end
end
```

24. Application of production P29:

```
begin [statement] ; [statement] ;
 while b_operand do
  begin
   [statement] ; [statement] ; [statement] ;
   if b_operand then [statement]
   else
    begin
     [statement] ;
     if b_operand then [statement]
     else [statement]
    end   end   end
```

25. ... 31. Application of production P22:

```
begin [operator] ; [operator] ;
 while b_operand do
  begin
   [operator] ; [operator] ; [operator] ;
   if b_operand then [operator]
   else
    begin
     [operator] ;
     if b_operand then [operator]
     else [operator]
    end
  end
end .
```

32. ... 38. Application of production P13:

```
begin
 system_init ( operator_type , [ operands ] ) ;
 set1 ( operator_type , [ operands ] ) ;
 while b_operand do
  begin
   out_prog_head ( operator_type , [ operands ] ) ;
   main_menu ( operator_type , [ operands ] ) ;
   test1 ( operator_type , [ operands ] ) ;
   if b_operand then
     image_analysis ( [operator_type] , [ operands ] )
   else
    begin
     test2 ( operator_type , [ operands ] ) ;
     if b_operand then
      patient_data ( [operator_type] , [ operands ] )
     else
      set2 ( operator_type , [ operands ] )
    end
  end
end
```

34. and 40. Application of production P23:

```
begin
 system_init ( [operator_type] , [ operands ] ) ;
 set1 ( [operator_type] , [ operands ] ) ;
 while b_operand do
  begin
   out_prog_head ( [operator_type] , [ operands ] ) ;
   main_menu ( [operator_type] , [ operands ] ) ;
   test1 ( [operator_type] , [ operands ] ) ;
   if b_operand then
     image_analysis ( program_scheme , [ operands ] )
    else
     begin
      test2 ( [operator_type] , [ operands ] ) ;
      if b_operand then
       patient_data ( program_scheme , [ operands ] )
      else
       set2 ( [operator_type] , [ operands ] )
     end
  end
end .
```

41. ... 47. Application of production P14:

```
begin
 system_init ( [operator_domain] , [ operands ] ) ;
 set1 ( [operator_domain] , [ operands ] ) ;
 while b_operand do
  begin
   out_prog_head ( [operator_domain] , [ operands ] ) ;
   main_menu ( [operator_domain] , [ operands ] ) ;
   test1 ( [operator_domain] , [ operands ] ) ;
   if b_operand then
     image_analysis ( program_scheme , [ operands ] )
    else
     begin
      test2 ( [operator_domain] , [ operands ] ) ;
      if b_operand then
       patient_data ( program_scheme , [ operands ] )
      else
       set2 ( [operator_domain] , [ operands ] )
     end
  end
end
```

48. ... 54. Application of production P17:

```
begin
  system_init ( process , [ operands ] ) ;
  set1 ( set_const , [ operands ] ) ;
  while [b_operand] do
   begin
    out_prog_head ( write , [ operands ] ) ;
    main_menu ( $M , [ operands ] ) ;
    test1 ( eoual , [ operands ] ) ;
    if [b_operand] then
      image_analysis ( program_scheme , [ operands ] )
     else
      begin
       test2 ( equal , [ operands ] ) ;
       if [b_operand] then
        patient_data ( program_scheme , [ operands ] )
       else
        set2 ( set_const   [ operands ] )
      end
   end
end
```

55. ... 57. Application of production P32:

```
begin
 system_init ( process , [ [operands] ] ) ;
 set1 ( set_const , [ [operands] ] ) ;
 while loop ( boolean , in ) do
  begin
   out_prog_head ( write , [ [operands] ] ) ;
   main_menu ( $M , [ [operands] ] ) ;
   test1 ( equal , [ [operands] ] ) ;
   if im_ana ( boolean , in ) then
     image_analysis ( program_scheme , [ [operands] ] )
    else
     begin
      test2 ( equal , [ [operands] ] ) ;
      if pat_man ( boolean , in ) then
       patient_data ( program_scheme , [ [operands] ] )
      else
       set2 ( set_const , [ [operands] ] )
     end
  end
end .
```

58. ... 74.: Generation of operand lists by applying P15 and P16:

```
begin
 system_init ( process , [ [operand] ] ) ;
 set1 ( set_const , [ [operand] , [operand] ] ) ;
 while loop ( boolean , in ) do
  begin
   out_prog_head ( write , [ [operand] ,
                             [operand] ] ) ;
   main_menu ( $M , [ [operand] ] ) ;
   test1 ( equal , [ [operand] , [operand] ,
                                  [operand] ] ) ;
   if im_ana ( boolean , in ) then
     image_analysis ( program_scheme ,
                      [ [operand] , [operand] ] )
    else
     begin
      test2 ( equal , [ [operand] , [operand] ,
                                    [operand] ] ) ;
      if pat_man ( boolean , in ) then
       patient_data ( program_scheme ,
                      [ [operand] ] )
      else
       set2 ( set_const , [ [operand] , [operand] ] )
     end
  end
end .
```

75. ... 89.: Deriving operands applying production P1:

```
begin
 system_init ( process , [ frame ( image , out ) ] ) ;
 set1 ( set_const , [ loop ( boolean , out ) ,
                      t ( true , in ) ] ) ;
 while loop ( boolean , in ) do
  begin
   out_prog_head ( write ,
                 [ frame ( image , out ) ,
                   header ( string , in ) ] ) ;
   main_menu ( $M , [ ans ( $D , out ) ] ) ;
   test1 ( equal , [ ans ( $D , in ) ,
                   ans1 ( $D1 , in ) ,
                   im_ana ( boolean , out ) ] ) ;
   if im_ana ( boolean , in ) then
    image_analysis ( [program_scheme] ,
                     [ frame ( image , inout ) ,
                       results ( $R , out ) ] )
   else
    begin
     test2 ( equal , [ ans ( $D , in ) ,
                       ans1 ( $D2 , in ) ,
                       pat_man ( boolean , out ) ] ) ;
     if pat_man ( boolean , in ) then
      patient_data ( [program_scheme] ,
                     [ frame ( image , out ) ] )
     else
      set2 ( set_const , [ loop ( boolean , out ) ,
                           f ( false , in ) ] )
    end
  end
end .
```

90. ... 91. Deriving operands applying production P19:

```
begin
 system_init ( process , [ frame ( image , out ) ] )
 set1 ( set_const , [ loop ( boolean , out ) ,
                         t ( true , in ) ] ) ;
 while loop ( boolean , in ) do
  begin
   out_prog_head ( write ,
                  [ frame ( image , out ) ,
                    header ( string , in ) ] ) ;
   main_menu ( $M , [ ans ( $D , out ) ] ) ;
   test1 ( equal , [ ans ( $D , in ) ,
                    ans1 ( $D1 , in ) ,
                    im_ana ( boolean , out ) ] ) ;
   if im_ana ( boolean , in ) then
     image_analysis ( begin
                       [statements]
                      end ,
                      [ frame ( image , inout ) ,
                        results ( $R , out ) ] )
    else
     begin
      test2 ( equal , [ ans ( $D , in ) ,
                        ans1 ( $D2 , in ) ,
                        pat_man ( boolean , out ) ] ) ;
      if pat_man ( boolean , in ) then
       patient_data ( begin
                       [statements]
                      end ,
                      [ frame ( image , out ) ] )
      else
       set2 ( set_const , [ loop ( boolean , out ) ,
                            f ( false , in ) ] )
     end
  end
end .
```

92. ... 98. Deriving subschemes by production P19 and P20:

```
begin
 system_init ( process , [ frame ( image , out ) ] ) ;
 set1 ( set_const , [ loop ( boolean , out ) ,
                      t ( true , in ) ] ) ;
 while loop ( boolean , in ) do
  begin
   out_prog_head ( write ,
                  [ frame ( image , out ) ,
                    header ( string , in ) ] ) ;
   main_menu ( $M , [ ans ( $D , out ) ] ) ;
   test1 ( equal , [ ans ( $D , in ) ,
                    ans1 ( $D1 , in ) ,
                    im_ana ( boolean , out ) ] ) ,
   if im_ana ( boolean , in ) then
     image_analysis ( begin
          statement ; statement ; statement ; statement
                      end ,
                      [ frame ( image , inout ) ,
                        results ( $R , out ) ] )
    else
     begin
      test2 ( equal , [ ans ( $D , in ) ,
                        ans1 ( $D2 , in ) ,
                        pat_man ( boolean , out ) ] ) ;
      if pat_man ( boolean , in ) then
       patient_data ( begin
                      statement ; statement ; statement
                      end ,
                      [ frame ( image , out ) ] )
      else
       set2 ( set_const , [ loop ( boolean , out ) ,
                            f ( false , in ) ] )
     end
  end
end
```

e.t.c.

*Appendix 2: Program construction example*

For specifying a refinement example, at first we assume the following operator and operand domain specification trees. In these trees, the complexity values $\chi(x)$ are given in its form

$$\sum_{y \in \mathbb{L}(x)} \mathrm{DISP}(x,y) / \mathrm{card}(\mathbb{L}(x))$$

The roots $\phi_{root}$ = *most_general_operator* and $\delta_{root}$ = *most_general_operand* do have the complexity values 85/16=5.3125 and 51/13=3.9230..., respectively.

We assume the following tree $(\Phi, <)$ which is a 'fragment' of a certain specification tree as used in a knowledge base for program construction in image analysis:

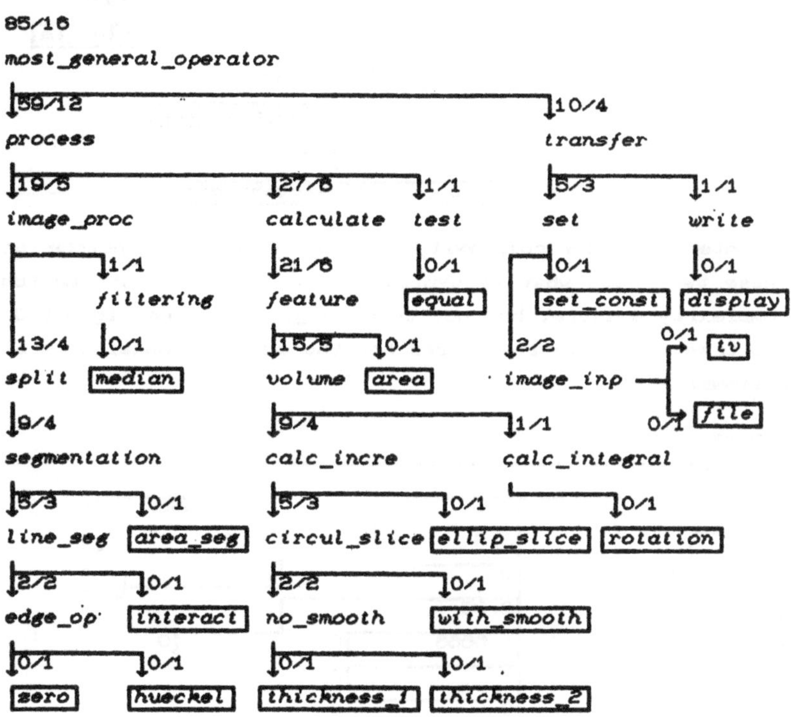

Also, the tree (Θ,<) is a fragment within the context of image analysis:

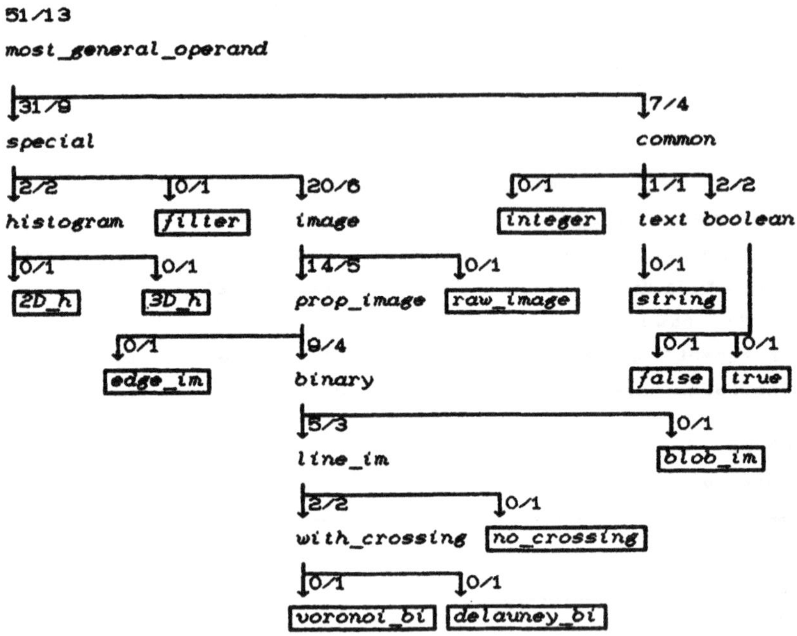


Note that the complexity values of $\chi$ are monotone on these two trees what is typically the case for this medium complexity measure, but not true in general, see fig.3.1-3. The tree of complexity values for the operator domains is as follows:

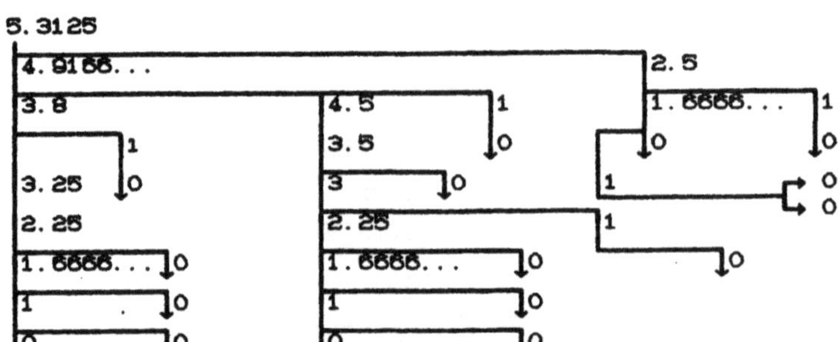

For the operand domains we have the following tree of complexity values in the given example:

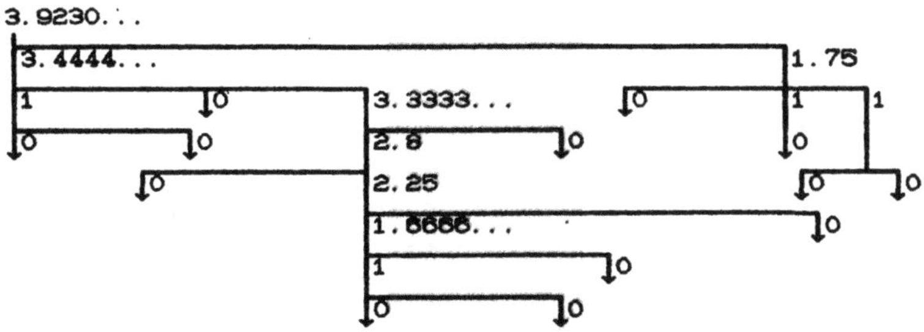


These assumed specification trees are sufficient to illustrate a typical program construction step following our general approach. Therefore, we also assume that a certain program scheme *P* and a certain set ℂ of global constraints are characterizing the actual refinement situation which was selected by the *FOCUS_ON_OPERATOR/OPERAND*-operator of the design space, where we assume that an operator refinement was selected as the next design space activity. The operator to refine is contained within the program scheme *P* which is located at a certain construction level *i* of the program construction process. The refinement of this operator leads to a program scheme *P'* at construction level *i+1*.

Now, assume that given is an actual program scheme *P*, where all the operator domains and operand domains appearing in 𝒫 are labels of the given examples of specification trees:

```
P =  begin
      system_init ( process , [ frame ( $I , out ) ] ) ;
      set1 ( set_const , [ loop ( boolean , out ) ,
                            t ( true , in ) ] ) ;
      while loop ( boolean , in ) do
       begin
        out_prog_head ( write ,
                        [ frame ( $I , out ) ,
                          header ( string , in ) ] ) ;
        main_menu ( $M , [ ans ( $D , out ) ] ) ;
        test1 ( equal , [ ans ( $D , in ) ,
                          ans1 ( $D1 , in ) ,
                          im_ana ( boolean , out ) ] ) ;
        if im_ana ( boolean , in ) then
         +---------------------------------------------+
         | image_analysis ( process ,                  |
         |                  [ frame ( $I , inout ) ,   |
         |                    results ( $R , out ) ] ) |
         +---------------------------------------------+
         else
          begin
           test2 ( equal , [ ans ( $D , in ) ,
                             ans1 ( $D2 , in ) ,
                             pat_man ( boolean , out ) ] ) ;
           if pat_man ( boolean , in ) then
            patient_data ( process ,
                           [ frame ( $I , out )  ] )
           else
            set2 ( set_const , [ loop ( boolean , out ) ,
                                 f ( false , in ) ] )
          end
        end
    end
```

where the operator

*image_analysis(process,[frame($I,inout),results($R,out)])*

is assumed to be selected for refinement and the following set of global constraints is relevant for this refinement of an operator contained in *P*:

```
C = {...,specialization($I,image),
     specialization($R,histogram),...}.
```

It is assumed that the knowledge base of the program space contains the rules $\rho_1$, $\rho_2$, $\rho_3$ and $\rho_4$ (as well as further, here not specified rules) with

```
ρ1 = (t1,c1,s1) and
     t1 = p(image_proc,[a($A,out),b($B,inout)]) →
          begin
           scan(image_inp,[b($B,out),c(filter,in)]);
           analyse(image_proc,[b($B,inout),a($A,out)])
          end.
      c1 = and (specialization($B,image),
                specialization($A,histogram))
      s1 = 'scanning of %b% and calculation of %a%'

ρ2 = (t2,c2,s2) with
     t2 = p(process,[r($D,out),f1($I1,inout)]) →
          begin
           scan(image_inp,[f1($I1,out),p(filter,in)]);
           preproc($T,[f1($I1,in),f2($I2,out)]);
           analyse(image_proc,[f2($I2,inout),r($D,out)])
          end.
      c2 = and (
            and ( specialization($I1,image),
                  specialization($I2,$I1)
                ),
            specialization($T,edge_op)
              )
      s2 = 'scanning and preprocessing of %f1% and
            calculation of %r%'
```

$\rho_3 = (t_3, c_3, s_3)$ with

```
t3 = p(calculate,[r($R,out),f1($IM1,inout)]) →
     begin
      scan(image_inp,[f1($IM1,out),p(filter,in)]);
      preproc($T,[f1($IM1,in),f2($IM2,out)]);
      analyse(image_proc,[f1($IM2,inout),r($R,out)])
     end.

c3 = and (
       and ( specialization($IM1,image),
             specialization($IM2,$IM1)
           ),
       specialization($T,filtering)
         )

s3 = 'scanning and preprocessing of %f1% and
       calculation of %r%'
```

$\rho_4 = (t_4, c_4, s_4)$ with

```
t4 = p(process,[a($R,out),f1($I1,inout)]) →
     begin
      scan(image_inp,[f1($I1,out),p(filter,in)]);
      preproc($T,[f1($I1,in),f2($I2,out)]);
      analyse(image_proc,[f1($I2,inout),a($R,out)])
     end.

c4 = and ( specialization($I1,image),
           specialization($I2,$I1) )

s4 = 'scanning and preprocessing of %f1% and
       calculation of %a%'
```

Within the problem space conditions $\varkappa_1$, $\varkappa_2$, $\varkappa_3$ and $\varkappa_4$ may be formulated with

```
x1 =and(
      (general_task = image_analysis)
      (quality_of_input_image = sufficient)
     )
```

$\varkappa_2$=*and(*

*(general_task = image_analysis)*

*(preprocessing = automatic_edge_detection)*

*)*

$\varkappa_3$=*and(*

*(general_task = image_analysis)*

*(preprocessing = filtering)*

*)*

$\varkappa_4$=*and(*

*(general_task = image_analysis)*

*(quality_of_input_image = not_sufficient)*

*)*

Such conditions are predefined situations which may be realized by specific sequences of answers of the user where the communication is realized by CDS's. Besides many other correspondences, the connection table of the inference machine may contain the following correspondences:

$$\mathbb{CT} = \langle \ldots, (\rho_1, \varkappa_1), (\rho_2, \varkappa_2), (\rho_3, \varkappa_3), (\rho_4, \varkappa_4), \ldots \rangle.$$

For discussing possible mechanisms of one refinement step applied to operator

*image_analysis(process, [frame($I, inout), results($R, out)]),*

at first we note that after the assumed application of the *FOCUS_ON_OPERATOR*-operator of the design space now the *REFINE*-operator has to be applied.

In its MATCH-phase we find that the operator domain symbol *process* is labelling a subtree of $(\Phi, \langle O)$ having nodes with labels *process*, *image_proc*, *calculate*, ..., *hueckel*, ..., *equal*. The rules $\rho_1$, $\rho_2$, $\rho_3$, and $\rho_4$ are mapping such domains onto structures and the signature of the premises (i.e. a list of operands) of these rules may be unified with the signature of these rules in each case, satisfying the set of global constraints $\mathbb{C}$ which was build-up so far. Thus, all of these four rules may be selected as applicable during the MATCH-phase. The set of applicable rules is called *conflict set*.

Now, in the SELECT-phase the connection table is checked what condition of the problem space does support the application of what rule of the conflict set. Assume that in the data base of the problem space, by interactive dialogue with the user, so far it was determined that a certain key, say *general_task*, has the value *image_analysis*. If there are no further evaluations of keys in the problem space having values *quality_of_input_image* or *preprocessing*, for ensuring a unique decision for applying one of these four rules, then in the strategy space one of the following strategies may be fixed:

(i) By interactive specifications of the next semantic complex in the problem space, a superset of evaluations is realized such that either a unique selection of applicable rule is possible, or there is at least a certain restriction of the set of applicable rules (e.g. *quality_of_image* = *not_sufficient* was determined, but *preprocessing* is not yet specified, i.e. rule $\rho_1$ may be deleted from the set of applicable rules), or all rules of the conflict set are recognized as being not appropriate. In dependence on these situations, the ACT-phase may be entered, further activities in the SELECT-phase have to be scheduled in the design space, or the *BACKWARD*-operator has to be activated, respectively.

(ii) Also, by decisions within the design space one rule of the conflict set may be selected for being applied in the ACT-phase of the *REFINE*-operator. Here, the complexities of the conclusions of the rules may be used, e.g. by the decision within the strategy space to favour the least-commitement strategy by applying the rule with minimum complexity for its conclusion. For example, in the case of rule $\rho_1$ we have:

Complexity of the conclusion of $t_1$ (without using $c_1$):

$$image\_inp.\chi + \mathrm{SIGN}(image\_inp.\chi)*k_{op}*(\$B.\chi + filter.\chi)/2$$

$+ \, image\_proc.\chi + \mathrm{SIGN}(image\_proc.\chi)*k_{op}*(\$B.\chi + \$A.\chi)/2$

$= 1 + \mathrm{SIGN}(1)*1*(3.9230 + 0)/2$

$+ \, 3.8 + \mathrm{SIGN}(3.8)*1*(3.9230 + 3.9230)/2$

$= 1+1.9615+3.8+3.9230$

$= 10.6845$

Complexity of the conclusion of $t_1$ (with using $c_1$):

$image\_inp.\chi + \mathrm{SIGN}(image\_inp.\chi)*k_{op}*(image.\chi + filter.\chi)/2$

$+ \, image\_proc.\chi + \mathrm{SIGN}(image\_proc.\chi)*k_{op}*$

$(image.\chi + histogram.\chi)/2$

$= 1 + \mathrm{SIGN}(1)*1*(3.3333 + 0)/2$

$+ \, 3.8 + \mathrm{SIGN}(3.8)*1*(3.3333 + 1)/2$

$= 1+1.6666+3.8+2.1666$

$= 8.6332$

Note that the complexity evaluation depends on the results during unification, i.e. the effects of constraints of a given rule have to be considered at least, but in general further specifications will be effected by the global constraints in set $\mathbb{C}$.

Assume, e.g., that rule $\rho_2$ was selected for the ACT-phase. Than we obtain program $P'$ at construction level $i+1$, with

```
P'=  begin
      system_init ( process , [ frame ( image , out ) ] ) ;
      set1 ( set_const , [ loop ( boolean , out ) ,
                              t ( true , in ) ] ) ;
      while loop ( boolean , in ) do
       begin
        out_prog_head ( write ,
                        [ frame ( image , out ) ,
                          header ( string , in ) ] ) ;
        main_menu ( $M , [ ans ( $D , out ) ] ) ;
        test1 ( equal , [ ans ( $D , in ) ,
                          ans1 ( $D1 , in ) ,
                          im_ana ( boolean , out ) ] ) ;
        if im_ana ( boolean , in ) then
           begin
            scan(image_inp,[f1(image,out),p(filter,in)]);
            preproc(edge_op,[f1(image,in),f2($I2,out)]);
            analyse(image_proc,[f2($I2,inout),r($R,out)])
           end.
         else
          begin
           test2 ( equal , [ ans ( $D , in ) ,
                             ans1 ( $D2 , in ) ,
                             pat_man ( boolean , out ) ] ) ;
           if pat_man ( boolean , in ) then
            patient_data ( process ,
                           [ frame ( image , out )  ] )
           else
            set2 ( set_const , [ loop ( boolean , out ) ,
                                 f ( false , in ) ] )
          end
       end
     end .
```

where the set of global constraints is updated to

$\mathbb{C}'$ = {...,*specialization*($I2,*image*),
*specialization*($R,*histogram*),...}

within the ACT-phase by deleting constraint

*specialization*($I,*image*)

and inserting constraint

*specialization*($I2,*image*)

into set $\mathbb{C}$. Note that operand *frame*( $I ,data_flow) was specified by *frame*( *image* ,data_flow) in all of its appearances in program *P*'. Altogether, this refinement step s characterized by the mappings

$$P - \rho_2 \rightarrow P' \quad \text{and} \quad \mathbb{C} - \rho_2 \rightarrow \mathbb{C}'.$$

Bei Fragen zur Produktsicherheit wenden Sie sich bitte an:
If you have any questions regarding product safety,
please contact:

Walter de Gruyter GmbH
Genthiner Straße 13
10785 Berlin
productsafety@degruyterbrill.com